Turning Skills and Strengths into Careers for Young Adults with Autism Spectrum Disorder

other books in the series

Independence, Social, and Study Strategies for Young Adults with Autism Spectrum Disorder
The BASICS College Curriculum
Michelle Rigler, Amy Rutherford and Emily Quinn
ISBN 978 1 84905 787 5
eISBN 978 1 78450 060 3

Developing Identity, Strengths, and Self-Perception for Young Adults with Autism Spectrum Disorder
The BASICS College Curriculum
Michelle Rigler, Amy Rutherford and Emily Quinn
ISBN 978 1 84905 797 4
eISBN 978 1 78450 095 5

of related interest

A Freshman Survival Guide for College Students with Autism Spectrum Disorders
The Stuff Nobody Tells You About!
Haley Moss
Foreword by Susan J. Moreno
ISBN 978 1 84905 984 8
eISBN 978 0 85700 922 7

Succeeding as a Student in the STEM Fields with an Invisible Disability
A College Handbook for Science, Technology, Engineering, and Math Students with
Autism, ADD, Affective Disorders, or Learning Difficulties and their Families
Christy Oslund
ISBN 978 1 84905 947 3
eISBN 978 0 85700 817 6

The Complete Guide to Getting a Job for People with Asperger's Syndrome
Find the Right Career and Get Hired
Barbara Bissonnette
ISBN 978 1 84905 921 3
eISBN 978 0 85700 692 9

Asperger's Syndrome Workplace Survival Guide
A Neurotypical's Secrets for Success
Barbara Bissonnette
ISBN 978 1 84905 943 5
eISBN 978 0 85700 807 7

Supporting College and University Students with Invisible Disabilities
A Guide for Faculty and Staff Working with Students with Autism, AD/HD,
Language Processing Disorders, Anxiety, and Mental Illness
Christy Oslund
ISBN 978 1 84905 955 8
eISBN 978 0 85700 785 8

Turning Skills and Strengths into Careers for Young Adults with Autism Spectrum Disorder

The BASICS College Curriculum

MICHELLE RIGLER,
AMY RUTHERFORD
and EMILY QUINN

Jessica Kingsley *Publishers*
London and Philadelphia

First published in 2016
by Jessica Kingsley Publishers
73 Collier Street
London N1 9BE, UK
and
400 Market Street, Suite 400
Philadelphia, PA 19106, USA

www.jkp.com

Library of Congress Cataloging in Publication Data
A CIP catalog record for this book is available from the Library of Congress

British Library Cataloguing in Publication Data
A CIP catalogue record for this book is available from the British Library

ISBN 978 1 84905 798 1
eISBN 978 1 78450 096 2

Printed and bound in Great Britain

CONTENTS

INTRODUCTION

At its most fundamental level, our intention with the BASICS College Curriculum is that each text serves as a practical guide through the transitions experienced by young adults with Autism Spectrum Disorder (ASD). The new independence in young adulthood requires the development of self-advocacy and resourcefulness, in academics and socially. Young adults are presented with the unique challenges of understanding their personalities and the strengths associated with who they are as individuals with ASD. Reframing negative self-perceptions yields personal awareness necessary for those who are charged with making serious life choices during the early stages of young adulthood. For individuals who have a solid foundation of understanding of both young adult practicalities and idiosyncrasies, especially knowledge of the basic nuances of social rules and essential academic skills, the next step is an intentional and focused one.

Preparation for the next move can ensure that the transition to employment or graduate school goes smoothly. From knowledge and understanding, the main idea in the first two BASICS texts, our focus shifts now to skill recognition and development, and taking preparatory action, first by recognizing strengths based on individual skills, and later by relating this awareness to job readiness. Developing skills and seeing how individual strengths play a role in the job search process is an essential component in career preparation. Shifting purpose from navigating new environments and reflecting on personal values to more concrete and forward-focused ideas, this text provides guidance through the fundamental steps of the stage *before* the job search begins. The goal is that with some direction, useable awareness of individual interest-driven skills, and the tools to maintain structure throughout the whole process, readers will tackle the next transition to the employment search with increased independence and resourcefulness.

Career readiness involves more than a college degree and a vague notion of commonplace industries. For many individuals, both those who have ASD and those who do not, acknowledging the multi-step process involved in career readiness happens as a result of dwindling time before graduation and the question, *what do I do now?* While academic pursuits do hold priority for those studying in college, especially if they enter college and build a solid grade point average (GPA) in general curriculum courses, students must also recognize that perfect grades mean little in the way of job readiness, and fail to demonstrate necessary experience to potential employers.

In our experience working with college students, the more focused and intentional efforts are during the whole of students' young adult lives, the more they are able to manage their responsibilities beyond the job search in terms of gaining valuable social and academic skills. Knowing this, our intention with this text is not only to guide young adults to understand the "big picture" of their career goals and to take reasonable steps to achieve them, but also to examine how they, as individuals with ASD, might struggle with certain job search process elements and provide strategies to mitigate these challenges. Readers working through this text will be challenged to understand their own work-related skills and interests, tasked to compile job search resources, and encounter discussion and practice regarding each portion of the multi-step job search process.

Essentially, readers will first work to investigate their strengths in terms of individual skill sets and how these influence success in the workplace. In the first chapter, they will compare interests, talents, and skills, and work to understand how they must be balanced to work together to improve one's employability. In Chapter 2, readers will specifically review skills and how to develop them as independent young adults. This chapter emphasizes the way skills are constructed from varying influences and how they can be transferred to the workplace. Finally, the last piece of identifying skill sets in a professional niche is covered in Chapter 3, which is designed to support readers as they seek to further understand their individual strengths as potential employees. This chapter culminates in a discussion of team-building reinforced by skill-based strengths and a discussion of how individuals with ASD can apply these as they explore their potential careers. Next, readers will craft visual representations to note their progress with elements involved in a long-term career search. Chapter 4 is structured to walk students through the value of the whole career process. Individuals will identify the pieces of the career-readiness process that fit together to guide them as marketable potential employees. Then, in Chapter 5, the text focuses on strategies for responding to realistic career possibilities and planning for the transition to employment. Networking and adjusting job preparation materials for specific job applications are key discussion points as students work through this chapter. Readers will also study and practice interviewing, job shadowing, and internships in the following chapters.

For many young adults with ASD, an interview might be considered a particularly intimidating experience. Chapter 6 guides readers through the steps involved in interview preparation, and helps them consider their options for disclosing ASD. After practicing interviewing skills, Chapter 7 will prompt the exploration of job shadowing arrangements, reviewing some social and communication rules that accompany them, and form a plan to request a job shadowing experience in the local community. Next, in Chapter 8 readers will connect their career readiness skills by working through the process of seeking internships that align with their interests and advance them professionally toward a career. Finally, in the last chapter, Chapter 9, we acknowledge alternative paths to success, knowing that not all people will follow a typical trajectory to employment. These paths for young adults with ASD might include graduate school, part-time work during college, or any number of planned or unplanned detours, all of which can be navigated with many of the same skills learned in the career readiness practice in this text.

One refrain that occurs throughout this text is an emphasis on the *process*. While individuals with ASD certainly have the intelligence and capabilities to achieve success in the workplace, simulating the forthcoming process can be a vital step during early adulthood to prepare them for the realities of the career search. Many students who go to college, regardless of whether or not they have ASD, struggle to take proactive measures for their future at a time when so much attention is demanded by the college experience. Despite agreeing that job readiness is a difficult process for most young adults, in order to dismantle figures that suggest individuals with ASD are unemployed or underemployed, our goal is that young adults with ASD actively work to frame their career readiness with the unique opportunities provided to them. There is significant value in the process of learning about one's own interests, talents, and skills, and applying this knowledge to job-readiness strategies. We believe that young adults with ASD have the ability to deconstruct the statistics of employment by obtaining and maintaining productive work that utilizes their education and suits their own interests and preferences, all the while offering an opportunity to demonstrate the vast strengths of individuals with ASD. Thus, this text is an effort to support the navigation of the complicated job-readiness process for college-aged individuals with ASD as they study and work in the transition to employment.

As in the previous two installments of this series, the BASICS chart will be the conclusion to each chapter to prompt self-evaluation. As readers begin the transition process into a career, it will be important for them to be responsible self-reflective learners, so completing these BASICS charts honestly and thoroughly is essential. Readers will have a visual representation of the subject matter that is to be reflected on in the same pattern for each chapter. While primarily providing a reflection on the understanding of the subject, the BASICS chart offers an opportunity for readers to perform a confidential self-evaluation. Following the self-evaluation, readers should be prepared to develop a set of short-term goals based on the areas of improvement identified through the BASICS chart. Ideally, the BASICS charts will identify areas of strength and areas for potential growth for each section of the curriculum. As students move through the curriculum, this process will help them become better self-reflective, self-monitoring individuals. To see an example of how to implement the BASICS chart, see Appendix A.

This guide is intended to assist readers through the transition of becoming a strength-based self-advocate. Professionals who work with people who have ASD can utilize the information presented in the text to facilitate discussions in a classroom setting, group setting, or individual meetings. Professionals can use the discussion points and questions provided in Appendix B as they see fit. The information presented is intended to be a starting point to be used with additional discussion, assignments, videos, etc. to best convey the information to specific student groups. Students using the text can take advantage of the questions and worksheets throughout to ensure a solid understanding of the topics presented. It is often the case that students benefit from consistent practice and consideration regarding new material, and we have designed the text to reflect this notion. In addition, the information in this guide can be used as individuals work through the transition of becoming self-advocates. Individuals can use this material and the guiding questions in Appendix B to move through this material independently or with support.

Individuals and professionals alike are encouraged to be creative with the material, and to tailor it to their individual needs. While the material is written to provide knowledge and information about the positive qualities and strengths of individuals with ASD, there is no limit to the ways in which the material can be utilized within a specific context, and this was intentional in our model. This guide is the result of research and was built on significant feedback from those college students with ASD who did not see their own strengths until after engaging in this work. As the true experts of ASD, these students have given us purpose and passion to help others with ASD see their own true potential in this world full of neurodiversity. We hope to provide our shared vision of opportunity and knowledge with individuals with ASD and those professionals who work with them during this exciting transition.

All worksheets marked with the symbol ⬇ are available for download from the JKP website at www.jkp.com/catalogue/book/9781849057981/resources.

Table I.1 Back to BASICS Template

B	**Behavior** 1 2 3	**Comments**
A	**Academics** 1 2 3	**Comments**
S	**Self-care** 1 2 3	**Comments**
I	**Interaction** 1 2 3	**Comments**
C	**Community** 1 2 3	**Comments**
S	**Self-monitoring** 1 2 3	**Comments**

GOALS

Personal:

Academic:

Social:

Chapter 1

COMPARING INTERESTS, TALENTS, AND SKILLS

INTRODUCTION

As young adults begin to plan for and enter the search for a career, developing a strong understanding of interests, talents, and skills will help guide the search process. By reflecting on these three distinct areas and identifying each, people with ASD may have more success in finding their place in the professional workplace. The first step in this awareness is developing an understanding of the differences between interests, talents, and skills.

- **Interests**: Topics or tangible items that an individual can study and discuss tirelessly, and that can provide motivation to individuals.

- **Talents**: Abilities that people are born with. These do not require practice or lessons to execute, and they often give the person a boost of self-esteem because he or she is particularly good at this ability.

- **Skills**: Abilities that have been practiced, studied, and developed over time. While skills may not be natural abilities, they have often been developed through repeated practice.

It is possible to view these three areas in relation to one another. If managed appropriately, individuals can base their major and career choice on the specific interest that is motivating. For example, college students who have a special interest in computers can choose a major based on what they enjoy studying. This interest can blossom into a good major choice, which can then be followed by infusing the natural talent of a student into the collegiate experience. That same college student who is majoring in computers can also possess a natural talent for observing details and solving problems creatively. This talent, combined with the special interest, could make the student an ideal candidate for a computer engineering major. Finally, when that same student develops a solid skill set that could include data analysis, problem identification, and persistence, this student could identify a career in computer automation design.

This career choice could allow for those with ASD to work every day within their special interest area, naturally build on the inherent talents, and will potentially keep them motivated to consistently build the skill set to allow for great success. While historically people with ASD are largely underemployed or unemployed (Walsh, Lydon, and Healy 2014), it is imperative to understand that the reason for this may not be as a result of an inability to develop or maintain a career, but rather a lack of understanding about finding the right fit. Everyone has a place where interests, talents, and skills can be combined to fit into a successful career. This combination can be referred to as a "professional niche."

LESSON 1: INTERESTS VS. SKILLS

Interests are topics or tangible items that an individual can study and discuss tirelessly. These interests typically vary between individuals, and can encompass broad topics such as world history or animals, or can include specific topics such as trains or flags of the world. For individuals with ASD, these interests tend to be restricted, may appear odd for the person's age, and can occasionally become compulsions.

Conversely, these topics of interest can also be very motivating for a person with ASD. It is human nature for people to enjoy doing things they find interesting. Children grow up playing games, watching television shows, and choosing toys based on their interests. As children become adolescents, they choose extracurricular activities and their peer group based on similar interests. The focus on individual interests tends to lose importance as young adults enter college and subsequent professional settings. Individual interests become secondary to academic requirements, potential career opportunities, or salary requirements. Instead of studying only the interworking of computers, a student with ASD in the US will also have to study rhetoric, history, psychology, and statistics as a part of the general education curriculum. The time typically spent studying interest areas must also be spent studying the required curriculum. Unfortunately, this is a time when young adults with ASD lose motivation for completing course work towards a degree. Without allowing time for interests and respecting the value of these interests, students with ASD could become disillusioned about the experience, and decide to leave the post-secondary environment.

Interests are just as important in choosing a major and career as talents and skills. They are what can keep a person motivated to work hard and to perform professionally while providing enjoyment and fulfillment in the career choice. Adults spend approximately a third of each day working, so it is vital that this time be spent doing something interesting and motivating. For young adults with ASD, these interests can become restrictive or they can become motivating; it is up to the individual to identify the helpful areas of interest as these can be the first determining factors in identifying the professional niche for an individual with ASD. It is possible to blend a special interest into nearly any major and career choice. Whether it serves as a break to re-motivate an individual, or is a catalyst for work every day, these interests can and should be respected as necessary tools for the individual to develop professionally. Career seekers should identify employers that respect and value various interests and talents (Grandin and Duffy 2008).

For an individual with ASD, interests may cycle through a variety of options, stay specific to one area through life, or may shift erratically, but identifying these topics that can give energy is the first step in becoming a successful professional.

Take some time to reflect on your interests. Ask yourself if these interest areas have changed over time, have remained constant, or shift frequently.

Reflect on what interests you:

_____

_____

_____

_____

_____

What makes this interesting to you?

_____

_____

_____

_____

_____

How can this interest help you professionally?

_____

_____

_____

_____

_____

LESSON 2: TALENTS VS. SKILLS

Talents are abilities that people are born with. These do not require practice or lessons to execute, and they often give the person a boost of self-esteem because he or she is particularly good at this ability. Individuals may naturally follow a path that is conducive to the talent they were born with, or may follow a different professional path but may use the talent to help them perform well on their path of choice.

Talents can be artistic in nature such as painting, singing, or acting. While artists work on their craft to build their ability, they are born with natural talent. Talents can also be grouped into athletic ability such as playing soccer, doing gymnastics, or running. Again, athletes practice and work on their abilities, but the practice is to build on their natural talent and athleticism. Talents can also be focused on academic ability such as writing, mathematics, or scientific thinking. Students study and do homework to enhance their natural ability in these areas. Finally, talents can also be focused on interpersonal skills such as communication, leadership, and problem-solving. These talents help people professionally and must be built on, but people are born with the ability to comfortably engage in these activities.

Individuals can develop the ability to engage in all of these activities, but if they are born with the natural talent, it will be easier to excel in the specific areas. People with ASD tend to be acutely aware of interests and may use their talents to perform tasks related to their interests. For example, if a person has an interest in trains and is artistically talented, he or she may spend hours drawing different types of trains to scale. Again, the talent could become an obsession, or it could be a motivator within the correct professional niche.

Unlike skills, talents are abilities that come naturally and do not require a large amount of energy to perfect. Individuals with ASD often display an array of talents that are used to demonstrate knowledge of the interests they possess. Skills could then be practiced and developed to enhance the inherent ability. Before these talents can be used to help an individual develop professionally, they must first be identified.

The four main areas of talents are identified on the following pages. Reflect on what others have told you regarding your natural abilities and identify those talents. If you do not see your talent(s) identified in the list, add them in the blank spaces.

IDENTIFY YOUR NATURAL TALENTS

Artistic	Athletic	Academic	Interpersonal
Drawing	Running	Writing	Communicating
Painting	Jumping	Math	Leading
Acting	Catching	Science	Understanding
Singing	Kicking	Technology	Planning
Dancing	Sports	Reading	Organizing
Comedy	Balance	Teaching	Collaborating
_____	_____	_____	_____
_____	_____	_____	_____
_____	_____	_____	_____
_____	_____	_____	_____

Talents do not follow a scripted path for individuals. Some people are born with talents from one area only, while others have talents from all four areas. One path is no better than another. It is important, however, for people to understand their talent banks so these talents can be used to develop an appropriate professional plan. Being knowledgeable about how your talents span the four areas can help you direct your focus for professional preparation. For example, if your talents are primarily focused in the artistic category, it would make sense to choose a major and potential career that respects and honors these talents.

LESSON 3: UNDERSTANDING SKILL SETS

Skills are abilities that have been practiced, studied, and developed over time. These skills are not natural abilities, but have often been developed through repeated trial and error. Skills are learned and fine-tuned through hard work and dedication. Individuals with ASD tend to focus for hours on interests and talents, but can overlook the necessity of developing a skill set. These skills are the things that can help people be successful academically and professionally on a daily basis.

People with ASD tend to have skill sets that are much broader than neurotypical people give them credit for. In fact, people with ASD have skill sets that are highly desirable in the workforce that neurotypical individuals simply do not possess to the same level. Individuals with ASD tend to navigate the world very differently than their neurotypical counterparts. This allowance and respect for how people with ASD view the world has allowed for the development of a pool of highly skilled potential employees who see minute details that are often overlooked by others, who can focus for hours on specific tasks, and who seek creative solutions to potential problems.

A separate skill set can interfere with the success of an individual with ASD as well. This set of skills is often referred to as soft skills. Soft skills include things such as communicating with others, time management, working on group projects, and understanding social cues. While these skills do not have to interfere with the potential success of a person with ASD, it is important to understand where potential pitfalls may exist.

On the following page, identify some potential skills within each skill set that you can commit to developing more thoroughly. As with any skill, it takes time, work, practice, and commitment to develop them. Some potential skills from each set have been offered as an example, but this list of skills should be developed individually with respect to your distinct experiences. If you do not see your skill set on the list, add them in the blank spaces.

DEFINING YOUR SKILL SET

Career Skills	Soft Skills
Attention to detail Editing Budgeting Investigating Problem-solving Training Focusing on projects Organizing _____ _____	Communicating Working in groups Social requirements Collaborating Time management Networking Professionalism Flexibility _____ _____
_____ _____	_____ _____

Now that you have committed to developing a specific set of skills to help develop your professional niche, you should also develop a plan for how you will practice and develop these skills. Identify people who can guide you in this development of your skill set and who can give you honest feedback about potential improvements. Identify resources, tools, workshops, and departments in your area that can help you develop these skills. Of all three areas necessary for developing your professional niche (interests, talents, and skills), this is the area that requires the strongest commitment, the most support, and the most hours of practice and development. With this third prong in place, individuals with ASD have great potential for professional success.

LESSON 4: CREATING BALANCE

To fully understand where a person belongs professionally, he or she must identify and analyze the interplay between interests, talents, and skills. All of these are important and play off one another. For example, a person with ASD may have a special interest in computers and be academically talented in technology and math. If this person develops a skill set of analyzing and documenting technological processes, he or she could become a successfully employed computational engineer.

Individuals with ASD often have tremendous strengths in specific areas, can focus for hours on identified interests, present significant talents, and have fine-tuned skill sets. Developing an understanding of how these three areas depend on one another and help the person fully develop as an adult can help individuals make good decisions regarding their future careers. By increasing the focus on skill development and building a coherent combination of interests, talents, and skills, individuals with ASD can find their own niche where both personal and professional satisfaction can be reached.

As you read earlier in this chapter, the reason you need to work to understand what you can provide to potential employers is simply that you must know first what you can offer before you can offer it. Further, knowing how to employ this range of tools at your disposal in the most efficient manner is essential to navigating the nuances of the job search process for students with ASD. Reflect on the lessons in this chapter and consider your primary interests, talents, and skills. Use this information to complete an activity to demonstrate how to maximize your professional niche using your unique interests, talents, and skills. For the first part of this activity, use the following chart to write one-word or simple phrases to describe what you can offer in each of the three categories.

CREATING A BALANCE

Interests	Talents	Skills
e.g. Computers	Technology	Analysing

The objective for this activity is to practice structuring your professional niche in a way that uses most of your interests, talents, and skills. For the purpose of the activity, the jar visual (Figure 1.1 opposite) will represent your professional niche, and uniquely arranged visual depictions of interests, talents, and skills will represent each piece of its contents. Your challenge is to arrange the contents in a way that allows for your interests, talents, and skills to be balanced.

Read through the notations for each category before you proceed with filling up your own jar, or professional niche image, on page 24 with varying contents drawn from your list of interests, talents, and skills.

INTERESTS

Your interests are represented by the image of a cotton ball. As interests can be compacted to certain areas of your life, be mindful of the malleability of the interests in your life, both professionally and personally. Interests can be shifted to allow room for skill development, and can cushion the impact of the effort this takes. Interests will fill the remaining spaces between talents and skills in the visual of your professional niche jar.

TALENTS

Talents are represented in this activity by the smaller round ball. They are not as malleable as interests, and do not take as much effort and commitment to foster in terms of your employability. Talents will need to be carefully added to the professional niche jar, thus allowing you to take advantage of your unique potential offerings to a possible employer.

SKILLS

Your skills will be the largest pieces in your professional niche jar, represented by the larger ball. Because skills demand specific development, support, and maintenance to be a benefit to you in employment, they will take up more space in your professional world than talents and interests.

Look at the example jar, filled with contents that present a student's professional niche, as it is balanced effectively. You cannot have only skills, or only talents, or only interests to maintain employability. For example, an interest in computers does make you an automatic candidate for computer engineering without other skills and talents that allow you to demonstrate your interests in a productive way.

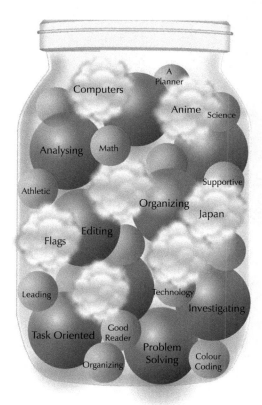

FIGURE 1.1 EXAMPLE OF A PROFESSIONAL NICHE JAR

Use the contents key and practice jar to consider how you would balance the interests, talents, and skills that you can offer to potential employers.

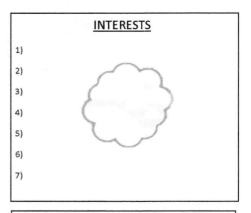

INTERESTS

1)
2)
3)
4)
5)
6)
7)

TALENTS

1)
2)
3)
4)
5)
6)
7)
8)
9)
10)
11)
12)

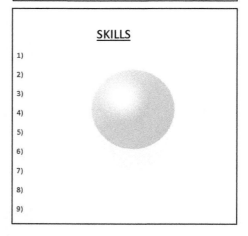

SKILLS

1)
2)
3)
4)
5)
6)
7)
8)
9)

BACK TO BASICS

Consider these guiding questions as you prepare to evaluate yourself.

B	**Behavior** 1 2 3	What is important about creating a balance between your interests, talents, and skills? How do you actively decipher the difference between your skills and talents? How do your interests motivate you? Have you set and revisited your career goals?
A	**Academics** 1 2 3	How have your talents been valuable in your success as a college student? Are you applying your skills to your classes? How are you balancing your course work and career exploration? Do you feel in control of your course requirements? Does your academic course work match your interests?
S	**Self-care** 1 2 3	Are you getting enough sleep? Are you eating healthily? Are you planning for your self-care activities? How are you maintaining an organizational system? What are you doing to make sure you are managing your time efficiently?
I	**Interaction** 1 2 3	How can you communicate your interests, talents, and skills in a way that others will see as positive contributions? Are you aware of your impact on other people? How are you monitoring conversations about your interests? Are you planning time for social activities?
C	**Community** 1 2 3	What are some areas in which you need to feel supported? How do you collaborate with others to further develop your skills and talents? What do others say about your talents? Are you willing to see the contributions others make to a team?
S	**Self-monitoring** 1 2 3	How committed are you to developing your talents and skills? Are you accepting critical feedback? How do you plan to continue to develop professionally? Are you advocating for yourself? Are you being respectful?

BACK TO BASICS: RATE YOURSELF

B	**Behavior** 1 2 3	**Comments**
A	**Academics** 1 2 3	**Comments**
S	**Self-care** 1 2 3	**Comments**
I	**Interaction** 1 2 3	**Comments**
C	**Community** 1 2 3	**Comments**
S	**Self-monitoring** 1 2 3	**Comments**

GOALS

Personal:

Academic:

Social:

Chapter 2

IDENTIFYING YOUR INDIVIDUAL SKILL SET

INTRODUCTION

As individuals with ASD begin the transition from higher education into the next phase of development, it is vital that they have a concrete understanding of skill sets. While skills naturally require time and practice to develop, individuals have an inherent set of skills that require less work to develop. These skills can be seen as a person's strength area when it comes to professional skills, and are the things that people can use to set themselves aside from others in an interview setting. Whether that interview is for a career or a graduate school placement, being able to discuss these skill strengths is as important as having the skills themselves. During any interview for graduate school or a job, potential employers will inevitably ask a candidate to explain his or her strengths. This is a time when a candidate can sell his or her skill set as what the employer needs to get the job done well.

If you were asked this question right now, what would you say is your skill strength that sets you apart from another candidate?

_____

_____

_____

_____

_____

_____

_____

_____

Young adults with ASD also tend to have specific skill sets that can set them aside from their neurotypical counterparts. For instance, one skill that is highly sought after in many fields is the ability to recognize details. This is an area where people with ASD thrive, often seeking to identify and connect the fine details that others may overlook when examining the big picture. This different approach of doing a task allows for people with ASD to display a high level of aptitude in careers requiring detail recognition, such as software design or IT fields. Another skill set that sets people with ASD apart from their peers is the ability to communicate very precisely. While social communication can be difficult, professional communication in a field in which they are knowledgeable is often accelerated. The precise communication skills of a person with ASD can be what make them good at writing manuals with distinct directives and steps to follow.

LESSON 1: ASSESSING YOUR SKILLS

Whether the advanced skill set is related to recognition of details, ability to focus on a specific task for hours without distraction, creating efficient solutions to problems, or communicating clear directions, many companies are beginning to seek employees with ASD. These companies are not seeking employees with ASD to increase the diversity of the workforce, or to be viewed as a charitable company; rather, they recognize the valid contributions that people with these distinct skill sets can make for their companies. It is an exciting time to be entering the workforce as a person with ASD, but you must be able to discuss your skill sets in a confident way.

The first step in this is to assess your skills and to analyze where your strengths lie. Assessments can help individuals identify the skills and characteristics they have learned as well as identify opportunities to further develop skills (Niles and Harris-Bowlsbey 2009). Skills required for efficiency and success can be divided into the following four main sets (see following page). While possessing skills in each of these sets is important to most professions, having a solid understanding of your strengths and potential areas of growth can guide you at this phase to develop each set as fully as possible. Each person has strengths and weaknesses within each set, but you can dedicate time and effort to strengthen each. This should help to ensure you are entering the appropriate career, you are creating your own professional niche, and you can communicate about your strengths confidently.

SKILL SET ASSESSMENT

Read through and circle each skill set and identify each that you would define as a strength for you. This information could be based on what others have told you or what you have recognized as a strength within yourself. Think about the tasks you complete efficiently and successfully in different settings (i.e. a group project). After you have identified the skills in each set that are strengths, note the total number of skills identified in each set at the bottom. This information can be used to analyze and define your distinct skill set.

Skill Set A	
Categorizing	Troubleshooting
Problem-solving	Data analysis
Researching	Evaluating
Detail recognition	Synthesizing information
Information collection	Comparing
Total for Skill Set A:	

Skill Set B	
Initiating	Memory for details
Time management	Focus
Prioritizing	Task completion
Emotional regulation	Multi-tasking
Planning	Task analysis
Total for Skill Set B:	

Skill Set C	
Verbal communication	Self-management
Nonverbal communication	Conflict management
Active listening	Making connections
Collaborating	Negotiating
Questioning	Consulting
Total for Skill Set C:	

Skill Set D	
Organizing	Coordinating
Strategic thinking	Delegating
Decision-making	Evaluating
Facilitating	Reporting
Giving feedback	Team-building
Total for Skill Set D:	

Using the numerical value for the total skills identified within each skill set, rank the skill sets from highest to lowest, and write the corresponding letters and total numbers on the following lines.

_____   _____   _____   _____

     Highest   Lowest

Reflect on the skills you identified as your strengths. Define how these skills could benefit you in your future career.

_____

_____

_____

_____

_____

_____

_____

_____

_____

_____

_____

_____

_____

_____

_____

_____

_____

_____

_____

_____

LESSON 2: DEFINING YOUR SKILL SET

The skills outlined in the previous activity were placed in specific sets to serve a purpose. A combination of these skill sets is important for every person to possess to allow for professional success. This does not mean that a person must be equally strong in each set, but every person must understand his or her own level of proficiency within each set.

Carry over the ranked ordered four-letter combination from the previous activity, and document the ranking on the lines below. This information will be helpful to have identified as the various skill sets are further defined. Read the definition and associated potential for career success for your strongest ranked set, and then follow with the next ranked set until you reach your lowest ranked skill set.

_____   _____   _____   _____

SKILL SET A: ANALYTICAL SKILLS

The majority of employers often require the skills within this set. These can include things that would allow a person to be highly successful in problem-solving and managing information and processes. These skills allow a person to visualize and analyze information, come up with efficient solutions, and make decisions based on logical thinking. Strong analytical skills are necessary to keep the workflow of any career efficient. If this is not your strong set, these skills can be practiced and developed.

Some careers that celebrate a professional with an analytical skill set could include, but are not limited to:

- Software designer
- Legal professional
- Data analyst
- Scientist
- Actuary

- IT professional
- Engineer
- Accountant
- Auditor
- Researcher

SKILL SET B: EXECUTIVE FUNCTION SKILLS

The skills within this set allow for a person to be successful in managing several tasks at once while being able to prioritize and multi-task and able to complete a number of things in an organized way. The high-level mental processes within this set allow a person to initiate a task, manage motivation, regulate emotions, control behavior, and sustain attention to see the task to completion. All professions require a level of proficiency in this set, and as with any skill, the skills within this set can be practiced and developed.

Some careers that celebrate a professional with an executive function skill set could include, but are not limited to:

- ER doctor
- Dentist
- Business entrepreneur
- Education professional
- Sales

- Psychologist
- Guidance counselor
- Office manager
- Executive assistant
- Writer

SKILL SET C: INTERPERSONAL SKILLS

The skills within this set include the soft skills that allow individuals to communicate clearly and to work effectively as part of a team. These skills can include things such as listening and communicating, questioning and assertiveness, and responsibility and accountability. Interpersonal skills rely on creating and maintaining balance within the skills and between the members of a team. The majority of employers will specifically ask about interpersonal skills in an interview because this skill set is very important in day-to-day operations. As with any skill set, these skills can be practiced and developed.

Some careers that celebrate a professional with an interpersonal skill set could include, but are not limited to:

- Family doctor
- Travel agent
- Real estate agent
- Public relations professional
- Business manager

- Investment banker
- Journalist
- Trial lawyer
- Politician
- Nurse

SKILL SET D: LEADERSHIP SKILLS

The skills within this set include those skills needed to motivate a group of people to work together towards a shared goal. These can include active tasks such as supervising, delegating, and strategic planning, but also includes much more broad and intangible skills. The abstract things that build the leadership skill set include things such as honesty, integrity, and confidence. This skill set requires courage and compassion as well as direction and commitment. Most importantly, a person who possesses this skill set is able to inspire others to accomplish more than they had planned for themselves. Skills within this set are highly sought after as they can benefit any person regardless of position. Leadership skills are often innate in people, but can also be practiced and developed in anyone.

Some careers that celebrate a professional with a leadership skill set could include, but are not limited to:

- Military personnel
- Coach
- Administrator
- Human resources manager
- Lead researcher

- Chancellor
- Principal
- Business executive
- College professor
- Consultant

Individuals have specific strengths and areas for improvement. It is very possible that the strengths lie in one specific skill set while the other skill sets are left underdeveloped. This could cause difficulty for entering and maintaining a career. As with any professional skills, if the focus is too narrow, there will be little opportunity for growth and development. Conversely, if an individual has representation of skill strengths throughout the four skill sets, the opportunity for professional success can become a reality. Take the information from the previous lesson as a definition of your baseline skill set. This is the starting point for your development.

LESSON 3: THE CONTINUUM

The four skill sets represented here share importance when seeking and maintaining a career. Individuals with ASD tend to have very specific skill sets, but these strengths, often in the analytical skillset, do not often cross over into the other areas. This has historically caused difficulties for people with ASD in gaining and maintaining employment. This narrow focus could cause people with ASD to have difficulties in managing the tasks and time needed to efficiently manage a workload, or in understanding and mastering the soft skills needed to work as part of a team. Unfortunately, a lack of strong leadership skills is often the cause for people with ASD to be overlooked for promotions in their careers. As reflected earlier in Chapter 1, the best avenue for professional success is to combine interests, talents, and skills to develop the best career option for a person with ASD, but the time needed to develop the other skill sets must also be taken into account. While the strengths associated with ASD can be the reason some people are able to obtain a solid career, strengths in the other skill sets will be what allow those same people to maintain suitable employment within that career.

IDENTIFY YOUR SKILL SET CONTINUUM

Again, use the numerical value for the total skills identified within each skill set, rank the skill sets from highest to lowest, and write the corresponding letters and total numbers on the following lines:

Scores:

_____   _____   _____   _____

Translate the numerical values for each skill set onto the following chart (Figure 2.2) (see Figure 2.1 for an example). Each section is labeled for the specific skill set. Plot the number of skills identified as a strength within each set, and fill in that section. This will give you a visual representation of the continuum of your skills. It is typical for a person to have at least one skill set that is much stronger than the others. It is also typical to have at least one skill set that is a weaker representation of skills. It becomes difficult when this skill representation is completely occupied within one skill set while the others are consistently weaker. This gives an indication that a person has dedicated time and energy to that one area of development, overlooking the need to develop the other areas. This pattern can be prevalent for people with ASD as they choose to work on the skills that come naturally to them and that fall within their interest areas and talents.

Skill Set A:
ANALYTICAL
Score: 8

Skill Set B:
EXECUTIVE
FUNCTIONING
Score: 2

Skill Set C:
INTERPERSONAL
Score: 5

Skill Set D:
LEADERSHIP
Score: 1

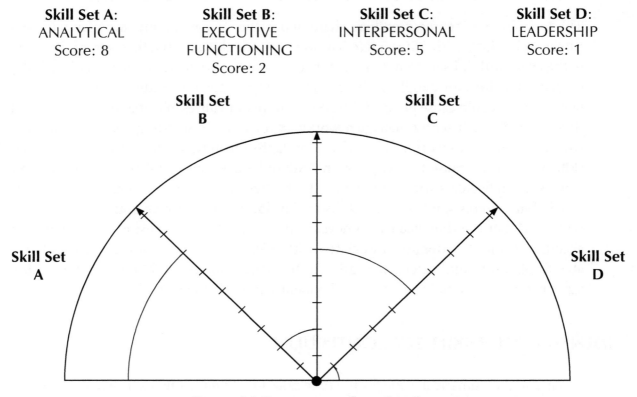

FIGURE 2.1 EXAMPLE OF A SKILL SET CONTINUUM

SKILL SET CONTINUUM

Skill Set A:
ANALYTICAL
Score:

_____

Skill Set B:
EXECUTIVE
FUNCTIONING
Score:

_____

Skill Set C:
INTERPERSONAL
Score:

_____

Skill Set D:
LEADERSHIP
Score:

_____

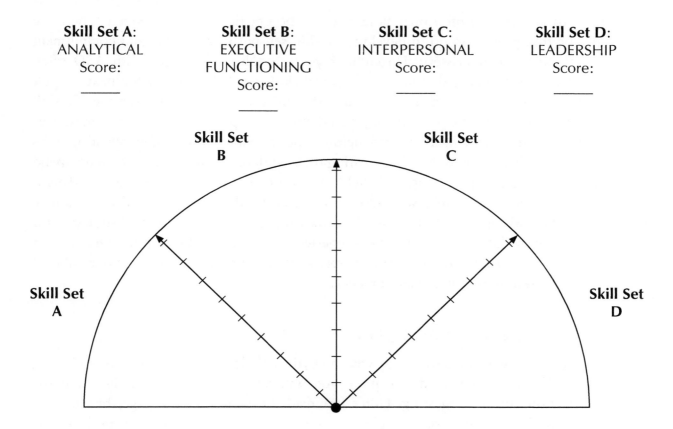

You can gather from this visual representation which specific skill sets you should designate time and energy towards to develop more fully. Throughout the next lesson, tips and strategies are provided to help you further develop the skills necessary to become proficient in these skill sets.

The proficiency levels in each of these sets may fluctuate with environment, tasks, and life experiences, and should not be seen as stagnant. Although one skill set may be an area of growth potential today, that same skill set may become your greatest strength as you enter your career.

Using social learning theory, Krumboltz suggests that through experiences in life, individuals develop socially, become self-reflection practitioners, and more fully develop skill sets as they progress through stages of life (quoted in Niles and Harris-Bowlsbey 2009). This supports the idea that we need to consistently be evaluating and re-evaluating our interests, skills, and values so as to avoid becoming stagnant in both our personal and professional development. With each experience, your skill set may shift, but your strengths carry value regardless of which skill set they fall into.

LESSON 4: CHALLENGE YOUR SKILL DEVELOPMENT

As with any skill, professional skills need to be practiced and developed. There are specific things you can do to develop any skill set, but it takes time and commitment to be able to gain mastery. Throughout young adulthood, people with ASD often spend time and energy developing the social skills needed to get to the next chapter in their lives. This same dedication must be applied to developing these specific skill sets. Athletes spend hours each day practicing their sport before a game, musicians spend months practicing their craft before a performance, artists often spend months developing their technique before creating their work of art, and college students spend years studying and practicing their field of study before entering their careers. This is the time when young adults with ASD should study and practice the skill sets that may not be naturally as strong for them. The following activity offers potential strategies for building each skill set. Although the suggested strategies may be helpful, these are not the only strategies to adopt. This is merely a starting point for building your habit of consistent skill development and practice.

SKILL SET A: ANALYTICAL SKILLS

To begin the work of developing your analytical skills, the first step is to read more books. The more you read, the more you will begin to think critically about the information you are ingesting. Don't just read the words on the page, but actively engage in the material. For example, if you are reading a fiction book, experience the plot from the perspective of the main character, and also try to imagine the plot from the perspective of a counter character. If you are reading an autobiography, read the story, but also try to develop a parallel storyline for what could have been if the person had made different decisions throughout his or her life. Finally, if you are reading a college textbook, choose information from each chapter and develop a method for how that information could help you solve a workplace issue in your career.

Another way to begin building analytical skills is to build your mathematical thinking. Spend time using the mathematical approach to problem-solving, but also break the process down into steps; identify steps in the process that could be streamlined and made more efficient, then develop a creative method for solving the problem. Practice the problems with the new method, and discover if your process delivers a correct answer. This process of step analysis will help you examine the minute details as well as creative problem-solving. The process of breaking a problem down step by step will allow you to develop your ability to recognize the smallest of details.

A strategy that may also help a person with ASD build strength in this skill set is to practice data analysis. Data can be presented in many forms. Whether it is written, spoken, or presented through media, it can be broken down and analyzed for correctness through an objective lens. To apply this strategy, a person with ASD could begin by asking the right question. In the beginning of this development, a question could be something that could be answered based on observation. For example, a college student could ask the question, 'How does the use of smartphones or other technology impact the face-to-face interaction of college students?' To answer this, the person conducting the data collection could sit in a busy area of campus, and document each person interacting with another person face to face vs. interacting with his or her telephone or other electronic device. The data collector should document not only numerical information, but also narrative data for what he or she is observing. After completion of the data collection period, the student should revisit the guiding question and begin to break the information down into categories to attempt to answer the question. Next, they should categorize and develop themes from the data collected, and begin to build details onto the data, creating the basis of the answer to the guiding question. Finally, they should ask whether the guiding question was, in fact, the correct question to ask, and then attempt to develop a statement to objectively answer the question.

SKILL SET B: EXECUTIVE FUNCTION SKILLS

To begin the practice of developing this skill set, develop a long-term goal that will remain the focus for no less than a semester. This goal should be both meaningful and attainable as this will be the first step in actively developing these skills. Identify what you want to accomplish at the end of the semester, and begin to make a plan with identified action steps, success indicators, and deadlines for completion. For example, if your semester goal is to obtain an internship in your major, action steps could include contacting the career services office at your school for contacts, developing an initial email template to send to potential internship companies, and developing a complete resume to present to potential company supervisors. Success indicators could simply be identifying which steps you complete on the timeline you have created. Monitor progress towards your goals weekly, document your next steps in your action plan, and celebrate any successes.

Another strategy and vital step in developing executive function skills is to develop a personal planning system to help manage the many tasks and requirements throughout adult life. Developing this system early, and modifying it as needed, will help you develop the habit of planning before you have to rely on it for professional success. This may seem like a waste of time in an already busy day, but taking some time in the beginning of each week to plan your week out in detail will help you be in control of your life. First, choose a planner that has a monthly as well as weekly calendar system. You can find calendars with rigid lines and blocks of time, or loosely defined time blocks, whichever works best for you. Next, on a separate sheet of paper, write down all the tasks you do each day. Include hygiene, meals, classes, work hours, club involvement, etc. From this list of daily activities, identify timeframes dedicated to each activity and document those on your calendar. Continue this practice with the other meetings, study sessions, dates, social commitments, etc. until you have planned for each event in your week on your calendar. Once you write an event in your calendar, you must also commit to adhering to your plan, recognizing that it is possible to shift times if necessary, but all things written on your calendar must be completed.

A final suggested strategy is to develop a time management system to help you through completing short and long-term tasks. For short-term tasks, use tools such as timers (physical or electronic) to manage the time spent on each portion of a task. Individuals with ASD tend to get lost in time while working on projects, resulting in far too much time spent on tasks that should be completed in a relatively short amount of time. This strategy could also alleviate the extended break time that often occurs when a person with ASD engages in something from their interest area to take a break, but the break results in hours off task. For example, a suggestion for managing time during studying could be an activity called "study power hour." For this activity, a student with ASD plans to study one topic for a solid hour, but that hour is broken up into specific tasks:

1. Set a timer for **5 minutes** and plan the tasks for the study hour.

2. Set a timer for **40 minutes** and work diligently on completing the tasks until the timer goes off.

3. Set a timer for **10 minutes** and take a break from your work, but stop when the timer goes off.

4. Set a timer for **5 minutes** to review what you completed, and set tasks for the next study session.

SKILL SET C: INTERPERSONAL SKILLS

In any school or work situation, people with ASD will encounter the requirement to work in groups. This task is difficult if an individual only identifies his or her own skills and strengths. An individual cannot fill all roles in a group and complete all the tasks alone; instead, he or she must identify skills in others that complement the inherent skills he or she possesses to build a strong partnership. To enhance the skills associated with this skill set you should attempt to shift your focus away from your strengths, and refocus your lens on the strengths of others. Begin with a group of close friends or family members first. Reflect on the communication style, work ethic, skills, and talents of the other people in the defined group. Make a bulleted list of the strengths of each individual as they would apply to a work group situation. Each individual will potentially have an entirely different set of strengths that you can pull from to build your work team. Now, using those bulleted lists of strengths, begin cutting the lists apart to build your dream team for work. Assemble the cut words into a new list of strengths and skills that will make your work group successful. Identify roles and tasks within the group to highlight the contribution of each team member.

Another strategy for developing collaborative or interpersonal skills is to build on the art of active listening. This may be particularly difficult for someone with ASD, but it is a skill that can be practiced and mastered. Some of the steps to building active listening skills include things like maintaining eye contact, staying focused on what the speaker is saying without being distracted, and reading the nonverbal cues of the speaker. These vital skills will take time and effort to develop, but with the right tools, anyone can develop the skills. Begin this work by enlisting the help of a conversation coach. This should be someone who knows you well and will understand why this may be difficult for you. Begin your work by facing the speaker as he or she is speaking. You do not have to make eye contact, but facing the speaker instead of looking away or looking at an electronic device will allow you to appear to be an active participant in the conversation. Next, listen closely to what the speaker is saying, and repeat the main words in your head as the conversation is progressing. Finally, as natural pauses in the conversation occur, ask questions for clarification. As you become comfortable with these three steps, begin to practice them with other people and reflect on the differences in the conversations when you use active listening strategies.

Finally, the best way to develop collaborative skills is to work with others to solve a real-world problem. Identify a community problem that fits within your interest area, and begin to enlist others to help. Develop a plan of action with members taking different roles, and create a solution to the problem. This community problem could be something within your family, school, work, or community as a whole, but should carry enough meaning for you to commit to the work. Keep in mind that when you work as a team, all members have valid strengths, opinions, and expertise. Develop ideas for solutions, but do not get stuck on your solution; instead, flush out all the possibilities and combine strategies from many suggestions to come up with the best solution to solve your problem.

SKILL SET D: LEADERSHIP SKILLS

Potential employers typically seek employees who display leadership skills. You do not have to be a positional leader, but you can lead in any situation if you have mastery of this skill set. These skills in particular will increase your marketability as a potential employee. As a person with ASD, once you become confident in yourself and in your professional niche, you should be able to develop this skill set to complement your professional development.

The first step in developing skills within this set is to first recognize which type of leadership you are willing to develop. People can be *vocal leaders* who give directives and encourage people to progress, *action leaders* who display the strong work ethic and encourage people to perform next to them, or *inspirational leaders* who encourage people to want to be very successful. Your preference as a young, developing adult may shift with experience and confidence, but defining the beginning of your leadership development is important. Research the various types of leaders, identify the one that resonates with you, and use this information to begin your practice of skill development.

Another way to develop leadership skills is to practice being an observant follower. Identify a person in your life who you see as a leader, and begin your research. Observe and document the things this leader does that are encouraging to you, as well as the things he or she does that may be discouraging. Once you have finished your observation period, categorize your data into themes according to how you would classify the interactions. These themes can be constantly compared and categorized until you get a working set of data that makes sense to you. From this data set, identify the behaviors this leader does that you would identify as positive leadership qualities, and document why you view them as positive. This can be your starting list of the leadership skills that you can start to work towards.

Finally, a strategy that may not only help you develop leadership skills, but could also help you develop confidence to be a leader, is to begin to mentor someone. Individuals with ASD tend to have a lot of great information to offer, but they also tend to have a strong sense of ethics. Serving as a role model for someone will help you emulate the characteristics in line with this skill set. Leadership is not based on tasks but rather based on people, so any practice you can have with serving as a role model or mentor, the better your opportunity to develop these skills will be. There are opportunities to mentor within school systems, the YMCA, colleges, or community autism agencies, as they are often looking for people to mentor young people. You can also mentor younger college students who may have ASD and who are trying to find their way through the social structure of college. Any information you can provide them with will be helpful, and you will also be developing leadership skills along the way.

As an individual with ASD, your skill set may be sought after for particular careers. As you learn to recognize your own strengths within each skill set, you can begin to further define the strengths within each skill set of those around you. This ability to analyze skill strengths can help you build a work group that may be a positive and successful experience. Recognizing and validating the skill sets of others may not only help you build this team, but could become a way in which you can build connections with peers and co-workers.

BACK TO BASICS

Consider these guiding questions as you prepare to evaluate yourself.

B 1 2 3	**Behavior**	How can you go about better understanding your skill set? How can you commit to strengthening your skill set? What are some thing you learned about yourself? What ways can you work towards becoming a leader? How do you interact with those who have a different skill set than you?
A 1 2 3	**Academics**	How can you prepare for changes as you progress through your college career? How are you managing your time balancing career exploration and course work?
S 1 2 3	**Self-care**	Are you getting enough sleep? Are you eating healthily? Are you planning for your self-care activities? Are you keeping your space clean? Are you making time to do things you enjoy outside of your academics and career exploration?
I 1 2 3	**Interaction**	Are you checking in with your support team? Are you actively engaged in classes? Are you looking for opportunities in your community? Do others see you as motivated? Are you checking your email/blackboard daily?
C 1 2 3	**Community**	Do you feel like you belong? Are you asking for help when needed? Have you met anyone new? Have others commented on your skills? Are you involved in anything socially?
S 1 2 3	**Self-monitoring**	Are you managing your time? Are you accepting critical feedback? Are you managing your frustration level? Are you advocating for yourself? Are your experiences contributing to your career goals? Are you evaluating and re-evaluating your interests and skills?

BACK TO BASICS: RATE YOURSELF

B **Behavior** 1 2 3	**Comments**	
A **Academics** 1 2 3	**Comments**	
S **Self-care** 1 2 3	**Comments**	
I **Interaction** 1 2 3	**Comments**	
C **Community** 1 2 3	**Comments**	
S **Self-monitoring** 1 2 3	**Comments**	

GOALS

Personal:

Academic:

Social:

Chapter 3

IDENTIFYING YOUR SKILL SET QUADRANT

INTRODUCTION

The first step in identifying your professional niche is to identify the skill sets that are strengths and the skill sets that could benefit from some practice and development. In the previous chapter these skill sets were identified and explored thoroughly to help students with ASD understand that each person has a skill set that is to be respected and valued. Individuals with ASD may have a specific skill set that is much more developed than others, and this valuable information can help these individuals find the major and career choice that fits best.

The next step in this process is to identify the quadrant in which the skill sets lie. Everyone has a preference for how they use their skill set in a work setting. They can be applied in an action-based method or used to strategically plan a process. These skill sets could also be used to lead a group of people through a project or to encourage teams of people to connect. Regardless of where the strengths of students with ASD lie, these skill sets can establish them as leaders in their career field if they truly understand how to best use their assets.

LESSON 1: EXPLORING YOUR QUADRANT DIRECTION

Once you can identify the specific skill set that is strongest, you can then begin to identify your preferences for using these strengths in a work setting. For the purpose of this lesson, the term 'work' can be applied to either group projects in school, research projects, or work teams as part of a career requirement. Those in a work setting cannot rely on knowledge and skills alone. There is a component to being successful in the work setting that involves being able to use your skills and knowledge in the way you prefer, that not only allows you to be successful in your career, but also allows you to be comfortable and happy in doing so.

To be able to advocate for your personal preference, you must first understand what that preference is. You have already identified your specific skill set strength; now you must identify your preference for how to best use your skills. Read the following pairs of statements and identify which statement most closely matches your preference in regards to working on a group project.

PREFERENCE STATEMENTS

Plan	Do
☐ I like to set timelines	☐ I work best under pressure
☐ I work best with a plan in place	☐ I like to just start the project
☐ I like to set goals	☐ The goal is to get the project finished
☐ I'm good at developing a vision	☐ I can follow a plan well
☐ I like to organize projects	☐ It is better for people to assign me tasks
☐ It is best to assign roles to team members	☐ Everyone contributes in their own way
☐ I use a good planning system	☐ I have a good memory
☐ I need to set guidelines for projects	☐ I like to be creative
☐ Measurable outcomes are important	☐ Task completion is what is important
☐ I like to clarify expectations in the beginning	☐ I like to just get to work
Total:	Total:

The information gathered through this activity allows you to examine your preference between being a person who likes to "plan" or a person who like to "do." The total number gives you an indication for whether you like to take part in creating the timeline for a project and defining the success indicators, or if you would prefer to get started on the project right away.

A person who likes to "plan" tends to think about the details of the project while projecting a potential timeline for completion and roles for each member. A person who prefers to work in this way tends to prefer guidelines and group norms outlined to alleviate any potential for conflict in the future. This person also values the process rather than the completed product.

A person who likes to "do" is action-oriented and prefers to get to work right away. A person with this preference may feel that planning the project is a waste of time and would rather just start working. The goal of a person who likes to "do" is often to complete the project as efficiently as possible. This person values the end product rather than the process of the group.

Both perspectives are very important in the completion of a group task. Whether this project is for school or for work, every group needs to have equal representation of people who prefer to "plan" and "do" to successfully complete the assigned task. If a group lacks a plan, the project will have no direction; conversely, if a project lacks action, the project will be have a great plan for success, but may never achieve completion.

Take some time to analyze the next set of statements and decide which one most reflects your preference as part of a work group. Remember that each statement is valid and necessary for the effective completion of every project. Base your answers on your personal preference for group projects.

PREFERENCE STATEMENTS

Lead	Connect
☐ I like to look for people's strengths	☐ I can identify commonalities
☐ I like to direct the process	☐ I like to partner throughout the process
☐ It is very important to monitor progress	☐ It is important to monitor communication
☐ I like to assign tasks to different members	☐ I like to watch roles evolve
☐ I feel better when I define the goals	☐ I enjoy developing the goals as a team
☐ I enjoy taking risks to be innovative	☐ Innovation occurs through partnerships
☐ I can communicate the objectives clearly	☐ I can identify progress from each member

Lead		**Connect**	
☐ I am confident in my ability		☐ I am confident in the ability of my team	
☐ I value the perspective of each member		☐ I value the linkages between each member	
☐ I can keep the team motivated to the end		☐ I can help build lasting partnerships	
Total:		Total:	

The total number in each column indicates whether you prefer to "lead" the members to effectively and efficiently complete the project, or whether you prefer to "connect" the interests, talents, and skills of group members to develop strong partnerships for the betterment of the group.

A person who likes to "lead" a group project tends to be confident in his or her own competency and ability to inspire the other group members to work towards the same goal. This person has an overview of the end result, and works through guiding and developing members to reach that goal. A person who likes to "lead" values the ability to inspire and guide, and may view success in terms of the individual development and growth of each team member.

A person who prefers to "connect" others within a work group tends to be very observant of the strengths and challenges of each person within the group. This person often likes to observe and take note of potential connections before becoming actively involved in the process. This observer often takes notice of similarities and differences and helps the partnerships within the team develop. A person who likes to "connect" values the relationships among team members and embraces the idea that a team is more than several individuals working towards the goal; rather, a team is a set of individuals with complementary talents and strengths.

Again, both perspectives are vital for any team to operate effectively. A work group needs to have a person who is willing to take the "lead" on the project and help guide the team through the process to completion. In addition, a work group must have someone who can observe the group and "connect" the members according to the best combination of skills and talents. Without a person to take the "lead" a group can become easily derailed from the goal, and a team without a person who can "connect" may have several strong members, but the end result could potentially be less than optimal due to overdependence on individual strengths.

You should now have an indication of your preference in each of these areas. Take some time to document the total number for each set on the lines below. You will use this information for the next lesson in this chapter.

Plan_____	Do_____
Lead_____	Connect_____

LESSON 2: IDENTIFYING YOUR COMPLEMENTARY QUADRANT DIRECTION

To understand how the skills and preferences combine to develop your role in a work team, an individual with ASD must first recognize that each person has value in a team. Nearly every career has a need for and requires the ability to work in a team. Whether it is required to complete a task, or the team is a permanent function of the job, every individual has a place. As a person with ASD, it may be easier and more comfortable to complete each work requirement individually. However, if you commit to only seeking employment in careers that do not encourage working in a team, you could potentially stop yourself from entering a career in which you could be exponentially successful.

While you have tremendous capabilities and strengths that are very specific, to be able to find your professional niche where you will be happy in your work, comfortable with your team, and successful professionally, it is important to recognize not only your role, but also the complementary roles of potential team members. Individuals with ASD tend to be most comfortable working individually, without relying on others to complete tasks. This often allows these individuals to work diligently to complete a goal without worrying about social confusion, potentially offending someone, relying on others to complete their tasks effectively, or becoming the scapegoat for task completion. However, this idea of working in isolation disallows the benefit of supporting others and creating a truly complementary team.

Each role in a team has its corresponding role that has equal benefit. While an individual may have a set of skills and preferences that make him or her a talented professional, without the harmonizing role to offset the inherent weaknesses, employers will not get the optimal performance out of the team.

It is your responsibility as a potential employee with ASD to not only recognize and be able to discuss the individual skills you have, but also to be able to communicate in an interview about your prospective role in the team. The ability to discuss this role and the impact you could have on the team can make you stand out as a responsible and efficient future employee.

ROLE GRAPH

Revisit the total scores from each subset discussed in Lesson 1:

Plan_____	Do_____
Lead_____	Connect_____

To identify your optimal role within a work team, plot the identified numbers on the corresponding X- and Y-axis, as shown, for example, on the following chart.

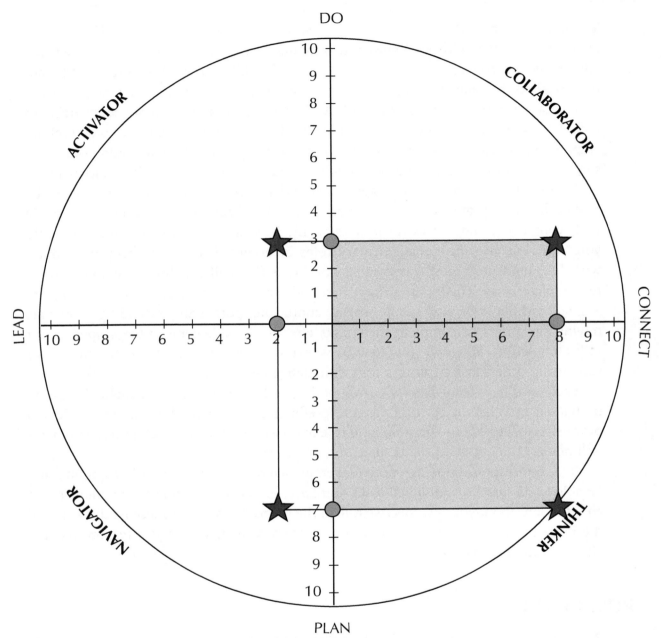

FIGURE 3.1 EXAMPLE OF A ROLE GRAPH

For example, Plan: 7, Do: 3, Lead: 2, Connect: 8

On each line identify two points that you will mark with a circle. Within each quadrant, graph the intersecting points with a star. Draw a solid line connecting each star to form a rectangle in the corresponding area of the graph. Make sure your lines also intersect with the interecting circles. This will help you identify your top two roles (shaded in the example above) and the harmonizing roles you should seek out in others.

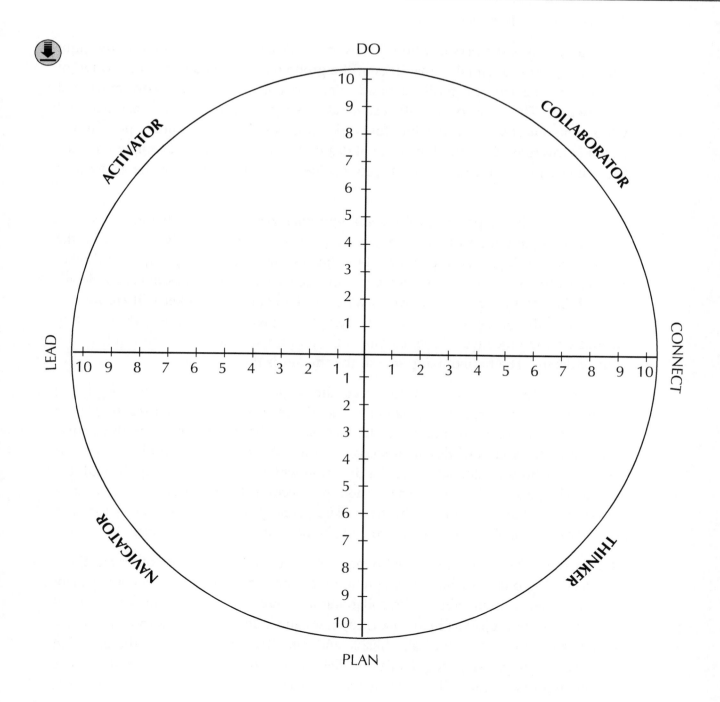

Identify the quadrant where most of your rectangle lies. This is your primary preference for your role in a work group project. This does not mean that this is your only preference or the only role you will play in work groups, but this may be where you are the most comfortable. The quadrant where the smallest amount of your rectangle area lies is your least preferable role in a group project. While this is the role you do not choose to take, it is very important to recognize the benefits of this role. This will be your harmonizing role in a team, and the person who fills this role will complement your role in the group.

If your star falls outside of the circle it means that you have indicated 10 on two areas. This is an indication that you are relying too heavily on that area and may struggle with flexibility in roles, and should focus attention on the development of another support role as well.

The roles can be described as follows:

Activator: This is the person who initiates the work and starts the group on the right path. This person often takes the ideas of the group members and starts the motion of completion. The activator turns discussions into action, and keeps the work moving at a steady pace. The activator will often suggest or assign roles for the team members and will outline objectives and timelines for work completion. Throughout the process, the person in this role will remind the team of deadlines and the projected completion date. The primary motive of this person is action. The harmonizing role for the activator is the *thinker*.

Thinker: This is the person in the team who analyzes all the information presented before making any kind of decision. This person often moves slowly, but will be the person who develops a solid plan based on the best interests of the group. The thinker requires all the details of the project, and will often spend time discussing these details in depth before attempting to move forward on the plan. The thinker will ensure that the work of the group stays within the designated plan and timelines while staying focused on the objective of the assignment. The primary motive of the thinker is to analyze details. The harmonizing role of the thinker is the *activator*.

Navigator: This is the person who directs the work of the team from the beginning to completion. This person may naturally take the lead on projects and set the plan in place. After the project is underway, this person may back out and guide the project from behind the scenes while encouraging other members. The navigator has a dynamic personality who is trusted and provides direction while steering the group through the process. The person who takes this role does not necessarily have positional leadership, but has the potential to guide the team. The primary motive of the navigator is to provide direction. The harmonizing role of the navigator is the *collaborator*.

Collaborator: This is the person who makes connections between the other members. This person encourages communication and idea sharing while giving encouragement to all the other team members. The collaborator ensures that all members are involved and active in the project as he or she recognizes and validates each person's strengths. The person in this role is typically likable and can effectively encourage the cohesion of the team. The primary motive of the collaborator is to connect team members. The harmonizing role of the collaborator is the *navigator*.

Identify your primary preference and harmonizing role in the lines below.

Primary preference:

_____

Harmonizing role:

_____

LESSON 3: BUILDING YOUR TEAM

For a team to be effective there must be a representation of many skills, preferences, and roles. For example, a sports team can only be good if each position is represented equally. If a team is made up of only a strong offense, they may be able to score, but without defense, they will be beaten often. The same can be said for a work group. If the group has several activators but no thinkers, the group will start on the project quickly, but may not be working towards the same goal. The thinker provides that direction, and is consistently aware of the important details that activators may miss.

One of the most notable strengths of individuals with ASD is the ability to recognize the details that others may miss. This strength would allow the individual to take an active role in fiscal planning, statistical analysis, research, or content analysis for any project. These are all necessary tasks for the completion of a large-scale project. Without a person who possesses these strengths, the team may get along well, work hard, and communicate effectively, but could potentially produce an end product that is not financially sustainable.

An additional strength that many people with ASD possess is the ability to make connections. Typically this strength is evident in the ability to make connections in details, but can be translated with some practice into making connections between people in the work team. A person with ASD can take on the role of listening to the ideas of group members and creating linkages between each idea, demonstrating the ability to expand an inherent strength to create a legitimate contributing role within any group project. While the role may be unexpected, individuals with ASD cannot limit themselves according to past success or failure. At this phase in professional development, it is very important to recognize that inherent strengths can be generalized into the work setting. Again, the key for making this successful is the commitment to practicing this skill.

Recognizing your own individual strengths and building on them is much easier than recognizing the skills and preferences of others in your team. To be able to ensure that there is adequate representation of skills in your team, you must be able to do just this. This requires the ability to recognize the perspective of other people, which in itself can be difficult for an individual with ASD. While it may be difficult, though, it is not impossible.

Again, by using your own strengths, you can analyze the other team members to build your understanding of their skills and role preferences. Just as you would examine the details of a research project or mathematical problem, use those same skills to identify the details in the interactions amongst team members. Take note of when team members enter conversations, when they become more involved, when they become animated in their interactions. These details can be clues as to the strengths, skills, and preferences of your teammates. This information can be useful in developing the perfectly balanced work group.

GROUP WORK SELF-ANALYSIS

Take some time to reflect on your skills, strengths, and preferences as they apply to work groups. Answer the following questions in your self-analysis, but don't limit your reflection.

What tasks are you most comfortable completing? In what roles do you feel most confident? What can you contribute successfully to a work project?

_____

_____

_____

_____

_____

_____

To make a work group most successful, you must be able to work with people who are most comfortable within your harmonizing role. These people would typically have strengths in areas in which you do not achieve.

Analyze your self-analysis, and identify the strengths you would need members of your work group to possess to realize the necessary balance.

_____

_____

_____

_____

_____

_____

LESSON 4: CAREER EXPLORATION

Young adults tend to choose a potential career based on college course work in which they have experienced success, the career path of parents, salary potential, or employment opportunities. Unfortunately, these same young adults tend to lose focus on what makes them truly happy. Young adults with ASD tend to have special interest areas that they feel passionately about. These areas can be studied and built on for hours without distraction. While it is important to build a career on what makes them truly happy, special interests cannot be the only factor in determining a potential career.

A responsible pre-professional would recognize and analyze all the information in the first three chapters of this book. It is imperative to use all the information you have discovered about yourself equally. Your skills are just as important as your interest areas, and your interest areas are just as important as your talents. The task is to find the career that embraces all three areas. This career will be where you can find your successful professional niche.

Other determining factors for choosing a potentially successful career path are to identify an ideal work environment. It is important to recognize that most careers have specifically outlined locations and environments for completing the work. For example, an engineer typically works inside using various technological tools, while a geologist typically works outside in the field. An insurance actuary typically works alone analyzing details, while an educator typically works in large groups making connections between individuals within larger groups.

It is also important to take note of salary expectations. While this may not be the first determining factor in choosing an ideal career, it is important to make the connection between your ideal living situation and the salary that will be needed to support that goal. If an individual wants to live alone in a particular locaton, it is vital to understand the cost of living of that particular location. This may help determine the required salary to support the chosen lifestyle.

CAREER PRE-PLANNING

You will more thoroughly examine potential careers in future chapters, but to begin the process of career exploration, brainstorm about your preferences in the following areas as they apply to potential career choices:

Interests:

Talents:

Skill sets:

Working environment:

Salary expectation:

Preferred location of residence/cost of living analysis:

As you begin this transition into the professional phase of your life, you will need to dedicate as many hours to developing your personal skills as you do to developing your professional skills. Neither of these areas can operate in isolation if you want to have a successful career. Just as you must recognize, validate, and build on your professional skill set, you must also recognize, validate, and build on the personal skills needed to stay employed. You must be able to work as part of a team and communicate effectively. Now that you have a stronger understanding of your own skill sets, you can begin to put all the pieces of your professional puzzle together.

The following chapters will help you outline your path to successfully entering your career, but always keep in mind that personal skills are equally important as the professional skills you will develop. Both require time, commitment, and practice.

BACK TO BASICS

Consider these guiding questions as you prepare to evaluate yourself.

B	**Behavior** 1 2 3	Can you identify specifics in your skill set? Are you utilizing your skill set daily? Are you exploring career options?
A	**Academics** 1 2 3	Are you managing your time, balancing career exploration and course work? Are you applying organizational strategies? Are you engaging in opportunities to help you identify your professional niche?
S	**Self-care** 1 2 3	Are you getting enough sleep? Are you eating healthily? Are you planning for your self-care activities? Are you keeping your space clean? Are you using your time management strategies?
I	**Interaction** 1 2 3	Are you checking in with your support team? Are you able to communicate your strengths to others? Are you looking for opportunities in your community? Do others see you as motivated? Is your harmonizing role creating a balance?
C	**Community** 1 2 3	Do you value others when in a team? Do you feel connected? Are you considering others' contributing skills? Are you utilizing your support team to help you get connected? Are you accepting critical feedback?
S	**Self-monitoring** 1 2 3	Is your energy equally distributed between career search and academics? Are you thinking of your passion and special interest as you work on your career exploration? Are you managing your frustration level? Are you advocating for yourself? Are you realistic about your expectations?

BACK TO BASICS: RATE YOURSELF

B	**Behavior** 1 2 3	**Comments**
A	**Academics** 1 2 3	**Comments**
S	**Self-care** 1 2 3	**Comments**
I	**Interaction** 1 2 3	**Comments**
C	**Community** 1 2 3	**Comments**
S	**Self-monitoring** 1 2 3	**Comments**

GOALS

Personal:

Academic:

Social:

Chapter 4

THE BIG PICTURE
OF SUCCESS

INTRODUCTION

When one considers all the components of a college education, including even detailed elements like how many hours are taken each semester, campus resource availability, academic preparedness from high school, and where students are in the process of career exploration, the greatness of a student's responsibilities can be overwhelming. Students with ASD can take advantage of structure throughout the later parts of their college career as they prepare to graduate. Students' focus during this chapter should be on creating a sustainable structure for career exploration. In essence, students will be studying some guidelines for exploring the "big picture" and learning from the process it takes to ensure they are marketable candidates for future employers.

When we refer to the "big picture," it is generally the idea that students will eventually need to have a job in order to make money to support an independent life as an adult. This is a minimal definition of "big picture," but students with ASD should be prepared to put some effort into seeking opportunities that increase employability in areas that are interesting, and in areas that allow for a demonstration of individual strength. For many students, this big picture will include some connection to the ideal career and lifestyle outlined at the end of Chapter 3. If students know they must work in some way to support independent living after college, it makes sense to pursue a job they would enjoy doing. In reality, though, students must be cautious of apathy at this time in a college career.

The students who actively seek opportunities to further their success beyond the academic realm of college are those who will likely be accepted to internships in fields they are genuinely interested in, ensuring that their work is both for financial support and also for personal satisfaction.

LESSON 1: VALUING YOUR JOURNEY

Before moving on to consider the logistical elements involved in career preparation, pause for a moment to think about how you want to define your "big picture" goals. Consider your personality, your values, and those strengths and skills you have identified in previous chapters as you answer the following question.

What does success mean to you? What is the big picture you are aspiring toward? Write down your ideas in the space below.

_____

_____

_____

_____

_____

_____

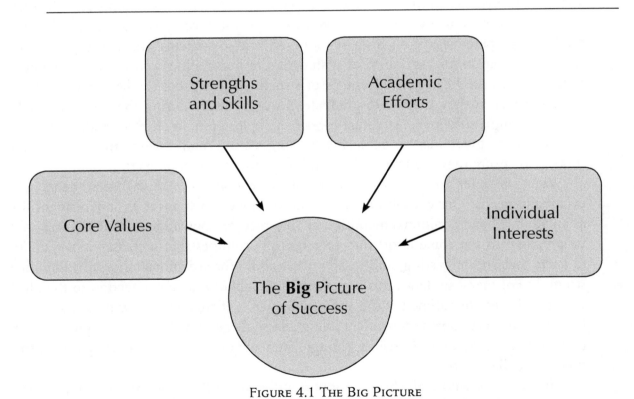

FIGURE 4.1 THE BIG PICTURE

Understanding the value of the career preparation journey, made more concrete by acknowledging the need to visualize the big picture, reinforces your notion of purpose while you work through this curriculum. One of the advantages that students with ASD often display is an adherence to behaviors in routine ways. You can take measureable steps to sustain your work toward your career goals by utilizing consistent and routine techniques to monitor your career preparation progress. One mistake that some college students make during this process is failing to consistently make an effort to gain opportunities to further their employment goals. Students make this mistake because it can be difficult to juggle the responsibilities of academic demands, a social life, and career preparation, which might include additional time commitments like internships or part-time jobs. As a student with ASD, though, structure and purpose, combined with your aptitude for routine diligence, can make for success in the career preparation process.

There are many smaller steps you will have to take to fulfill the big picture, and you may find it helpful to support your own efforts to prepare for postgraduation goals by maintaining accountability to yourself and those with whom you work through compiling notes on your routine progress. This kind of "checkpoint" system for the smaller steps can build some customizable structure for you that will guide your decisions and eventually lead you to employment opportunities. Skills take time to develop. You will need to fine-tune your skill set strengths, of course, but you will also need to practice skills that challenge you. In order to expand your skill sets, you will need to identify some skills that challenge you or that you wish to develop more competently, practice the skills, and monitor your progress. Consider what you know from Chapter 3 about your skill set quadrant to guide your skill progress reflection.

As you navigate college classes, your social life, and your other responsibilities and interests, keeping track of your skill development and how you are progressing in this area can provide structure to an otherwise potentially overwhelming set of tasks. Take a look at the example of a Skill Development Checkpoint System below regarding academic communication skill development.

This outlines the types of communication involved with the skill to be developed, and highlights the actions that can lead to the desirable outcome. Here, email is the first type of communication a student needs to develop, so the task list for email simply includes notes to remind the student to check and respond to email three times a day. The student would be able to check off the times he or she has responded to emails, and, with time, establish a healthy habit regarding email communication. Additionally, if the student consistently uses the checkpoint system, he or she would be able to notice patterns in the skill development process, like frequent disregard for checking email specifically in the mornings, such that these behaviors can then be identified and addressed.

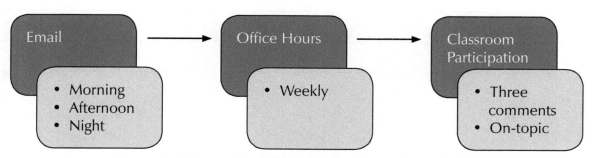

FIGURE 4.2 EXAMPLE OF A SKILL DEVELOPMENT CHECKPOINT SYSTEM

Now that you have viewed this example, spend some time creating your own. Start now by jotting down some ideas in response to the following questions that you can use to guide you as you create your own Skill Development Checkpoint System.

What is a skill that you need to develop in terms of your future career goals? (i.e., communication, interpersonal interactions, a specific industry skill necessary for employment, etc.)

_____

_____

_____

Why do you need to improve this skill?

_____

_____

_____

What are some barriers to your ability to develop the skill? (i.e., accountability, logistic concerns, etc.)

_____

_____

_____

How long are you prepared to work on a certain skill? (i.e., one week, a year, until it is mastered, etc.)

_____

_____

_____

What actions do you need to take to develop the skill? Are there specific steps you will need to take?

_____

_____

_____

Who can support you during the skill development process? (i.e., a mentor, college support personnel, parents, etc.)

_____

_____

_____

How do you prefer to monitor your progress? (i.e., a written chart, typed checklist, cell phone app, etc.)

_____

_____

_____

Note that there any many ways to keep track of your progress with certain skills. Your Skill Development Checkpoint System may look quite different from the example provided. In fact, you may wish to use your cell phone or a computer program to fulfill the same purpose, but for now, spend some time working through your ideas about the structure of your checkpoint system.

Three simple outlines are provided to get you started, so you can use that space to write in your checkpoint elements, or come up with a different way to hold yourself accountable to your goals. The most important element of creating your own system is that you create something that you will actually use. Bookmark this page in your text and remember to frequently update your progress. Be sure to include flexibility for additional points of progress to come. For example, if you are working on developing your computer skills, use one checkpoint system for that purpose, but be distinctive about any other skills you are working on, like making eye contact during a conversation.

SKILL DEVELOPMENT CHECKPOINT SYSTEM

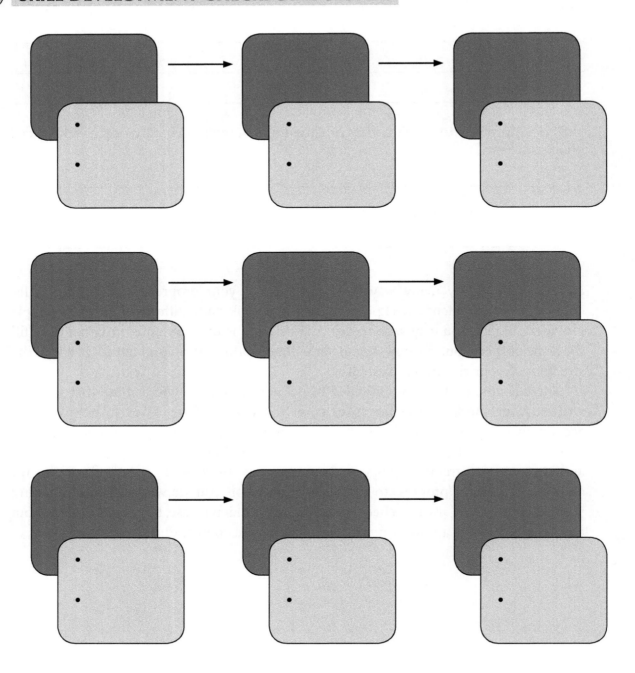

Learning how to visualize the big picture and the many steps involved in its fulfillment is an important part of valuing your career preparation journey. The process itself can teach you, in addition to many other things, how to set up a skill development checkpoint system that utilizes your strengths as you work through college toward your big picture goals. Having direction and guidance and adhering to the routine checkpoint steps allows you to experience college and this process to its fullest without ending up completely overwhelmed. In the next lesson you will take some time to deconstruct the "big picture" in order to identify the aspects of the career preparation process that demand your attention and efforts.

LESSON 2: CAREER PREPARATION, ONE PIECE AT A TIME

If you think of the career preparation process like a jigsaw puzzle, you can visualize the necessary components to the process as they create the whole image. This lesson emphasizes puzzle imagery throughout, and it is important that you understand that while this text discusses some commonly used components to a career puzzle, not every individual will fill every component of the puzzle, and some might have different categories that they need to fill for their career goals. If you consider the way you might complete a puzzle, you might begin by examining all of the pieces. This step usually occurs before you even begin to place the pieces together. So, we will first take a look at the components we will discuss further in this lesson. You will work with most of these in various other chapters throughout the rest of the book. For now, just read through the descriptions of the career puzzle pieces you will study in this chapter, and take notes if you make connections with these categories and your current career preparation experience.

1. Complete general education requirements: To graduate, most universities and colleges require that you take, and pass, a certain set curriculum in addition to your major-focused courses. General education requirements usually include a few classes that are not as interesting to you as courses related to your academic major.

    Notes:

    _____

    _____

    _____

2. Volunteer: Employers can consider your volunteer experience as evidence of community commitment. Doing something just to help makes a statement about personal character that employers find desirable.

    Notes:

    _____

    _____

    _____

3. Work experience: Any experience you have and can gain working, whether it is self-employment or with a business or service, is valuable to your career.

    Notes:

    _____

    _____

    _____

4. Faculty mentor: Connecting with a faculty member who shares your academic interests can be a rewarding partnership for your future, as they can help you navigate the field you have chosen to study and introduce you to many interest-driven opportunities.

   Notes:

   _____

   _____

   _____

5. Career fair: Most campuses, and sometimes surrounding communities, hold annual or semi-annual career fairs. Attending a career fair provides you with necessary networking practice in a structured environment. Career fairs give you a chance to ask questions about potential careers in a more casual setting than a formal interview.

   Notes:

   _____

   _____

   _____

6. Job shadowing: Observing someone doing what you are aspiring to do in the natural setting can give you valuable insight into the realities of the particular work environment. You can also use job shadowing as a chance to learn specific soft skills as they are modeled in the workplace.

   Notes:

   _____

   _____

   _____

7. Campus organizations and events: Employers can learn quite a lot about you and your work and personal interests from knowing about your involvement on your college campus. Campus involvement can include interesting clubs, work study, outdoor trips, or other university-affiliated events or organizations.

   Notes:

   _____

   _____

   _____

8. Interviews: For young adults with ASD, the interview might be the most challenging aspect of the career preparation process. Practicing how to navigate the nuances of interviewing can help you identify your interviewing strengths and weaknesses in order to improve.

    Notes:

    _____

    _____

    _____

9. Networking: Connecting with people in the field you are interested in can have a significant influence on your career. Conferences, professional development workshops, and professional membership meetings are great places to network and talk to like-minded people about your career field.

    Notes:

    _____

    _____

    _____

10. Interest/skill/major match: Making the most of your career opportunities can include making informed decisions based on your interests, your skills, and how these work with your academic major at college to prepare you for the workplace. It is generally easier to find that your major and interests align, but it is important to consider the big picture of a particular field, and where you stand in terms of the necessary skill development.

    Notes:

    _____

    _____

    _____

11. Related work experience: The most important work experience you can have during college and as you prepare for your future career is that which is related to your career pursuits. All work experience is valuable, but taking advantage of work opportunities that can further your marketability is one of the key elements of the career process.

    Notes:

    _____

    _____

    _____

12. Academic major: Your academic major in college should be interesting, of course, but you should also have some knowledge of career options for individuals who pursue your degree. There are resources at college to help you choose a major and to help you prepare for a career related to that major.

    Notes:

    _____

    _____

    _____

13. Earn a degree: Completing all requirements for a college degree will provide you with applicable knowledge of an interesting field, and may include credit-bearing internship or field observation hours. Employers may require certain college degrees for advanced positions.

    Notes:

    _____

    _____

    _____

14. Professional mentor: A professional mentor can guide you through important phases of your career preparation. A professional mentor can facilitate your professional development and offer insight into the field you wish to enter. Many college students seek out professional mentors from individuals who are not only successful in their field, but also have an understanding of ASD.

    Notes:

    _____

    _____

    _____

15. Internship: An internship in your field of interest can lead to on-site experiences that demonstrate realistic characteristics of the type of work you might find yourself doing in the future. Some are paid and some are not, but all internships allow you to develop a sense for the job responsibilities relevant to your field.

    Notes:

    _____

    _____

    _____

16. Resume development: Creating a resume, which succinctly comprises your educational, work, and professional experience, is a fundamental step as you prepare to apply for jobs in your field.

Notes:

_____

_____

_____

The elements listed here can also be understood as a kind of hands-on resume development. In the next chapter you will begin to build your own resume, using the puzzle pieces and their information to help guide you.

Take a look at the example of a young adult student's Career Preparation Puzzle on the following page. You will see that many of the puzzle pieces are filled in with career preparation components, but also that some are not. Most young adults, if they were to complete a Career Preparation Puzzle, would find that they do not yet have all of the pieces. While all components can work well together to illustrate any certain ideal career for you, not all 16 components must be filled in order to prepare for a successful career. Think of these pieces as some foundational career preparation elements that can help you along in the process.

If you have access to a puzzle, feel free to complete the following activity using a marker on actual cardboard puzzle pieces. Otherwise, take some time now to complete your own Career Preparation Puzzle using the template on page 73. For each career element you have experience with, briefly describe your experience with the corresponding label. Refer to the summaries you read previously in this lesson, and do research on your own if necessary to understand the 16 labeled spaces. When you have finished your work with all the applicable career preparation elements, you can then reflect on the missing pieces.

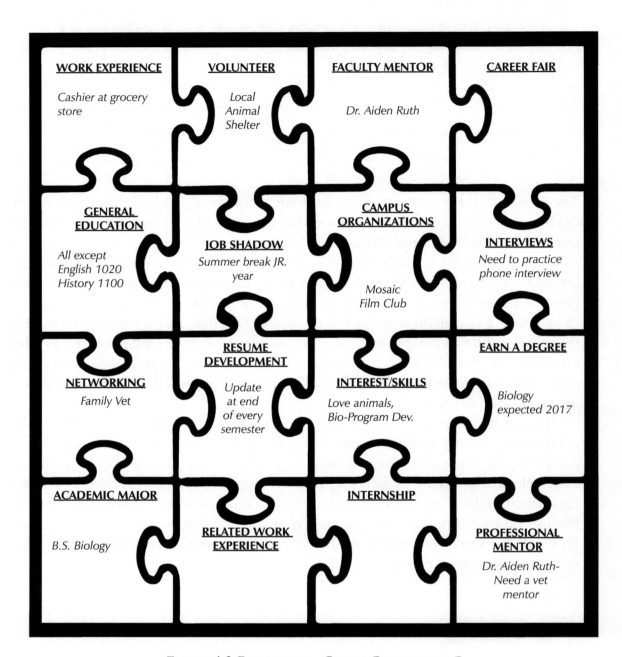

WORK EXPERIENCE

Cashier at grocery store

VOLUNTEER

Local Animal Shelter

FACULTY MENTOR

Dr. Aiden Ruth

CAREER FAIR

GENERAL EDUCATION

All except English 1020 History 1100

JOB SHADOW

Summer break JR. year

CAMPUS ORGANIZATIONS

Mosaic Film Club

INTERVIEWS

Need to practice phone interview

NETWORKING

Family Vet

RESUME DEVELOPMENT

Update at end of every semester

INTEREST/SKILLS

Love animals, Bio-Program Dev.

EARN A DEGREE

Biology expected 2017

ACADEMIC MAJOR

B.S. Biology

RELATED WORK EXPERIENCE

INTERNSHIP

PROFESSIONAL MENTOR

Dr. Aiden Ruth- Need a vet mentor

FIGURE 4.3 EXAMPLE OF A CAREER PREPARATION PUZZLE

CAREER PREPARATION PUZZLE

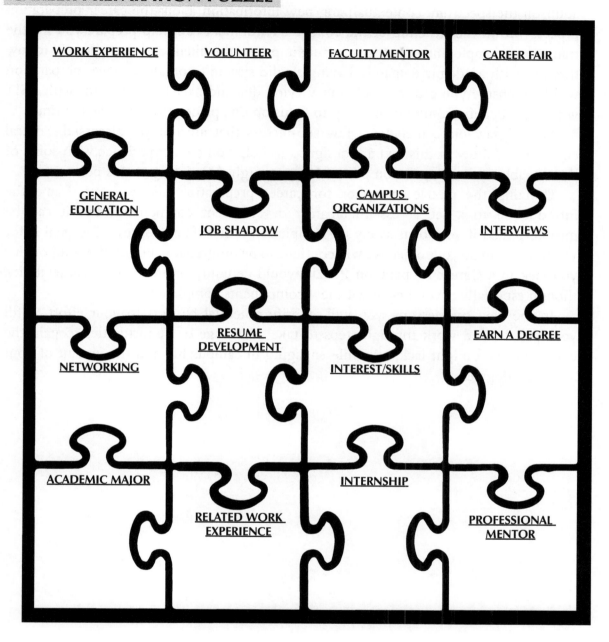

Individuals with ASD can struggle with disarray in routine and structure. As a young adult on the spectrum, contextualizing new information about the career preparation process within the structure of the college environment can help prepare you for the transition to employment. Just as structure improves the likelihood that you will follow through with academic demands, having a solid system to organize career preparation will help ensure you can meet all your varying demands. As a young adult with ASD, you might benefit from remembering to focus on one piece of the puzzle at a time.

Each jigsaw piece includes a few sub-factors that are not yet discussed. Several chapters to follow in this text are designed to help you gain experience with some of the valuable career preparation pieces that you might be missing at this point.

Utilizing the puzzle metaphor for career preparation allows us to frame the introduction to a set of essential career development components, but it can be misinterpreted if you focus solely on completion rather than progress. The goal is for you to develop, so your objective will continue to be progression. Filling the components you lack in a Career Preparation Puzzle would certainly improve your marketability, though especially if you began with few components completed.

In the next two lessons, you will identify potential barriers to your effort to fill your puzzle, and work through steps to take advantage of opportunities to gain the experience you might lack, all while engaging in campus life and the pursuit of your academic degree.

LESSON 3: MAKING SENSE OF THE PUZZLING DIRECTIONS

Now that you have identified where you are in terms of achieving some common career development goals, like those labeling the 16 puzzle pieces from the previous lesson, you can begin to outline your next steps. Transition periods can be difficult for individuals with ASD, and especially so when they bring about new territory in conjunction with increasing academic demands. Young adults in the beginning stages of the career preparation progress, which is generally rather exploratory in nature, can transition more smoothly to the more demanding process of actively seeking career development in a focused interest area with the support of structured models to serve as guides, and an awareness of available resources on most college campuses.

While there are certainly some commonplace standards for career development, including some of those discussed in this chapter, the best practices for crafting your own career development plan in the most efficient way possible are difficult to simulate. Young adults with ASD offer numerous strengths and skill sets to potential employers, but as someone who may need more direct instruction in a niche area of social skills, perhaps, you can benefit from taking extra care to supplement your academic work at college with additional practice in developing skills that your future career might engage. Acknowledging how your environment and the influential people in your life can contribute to your unique path will be the initial step as you set out to pursue career opportunities. Furthermore, in an effort to address the presence of increased stress, which is not necessarily a condition reserved for those with ASD during career preparation, it is important that you plan ahead for your reactions to the new input you are going to have to process. Some of the most important and consequential decisions are made during this period of a young adult's life. Preparing for some degree of inevitable confusion can only help you maintain a professional disposition as you are dealt your share of responsible decisions.

Before you work through this lesson's activity to compile resources to assist your professional development, take some time to consider a few influential factors that you will address in your construction of your career plan. You have already explored some of these elements in the first lesson when you positioned yourself in your big picture of success. Here are a few reflection questions to help guide your thoughts as you work to express how your environment and progress contribute to your status as a potential employee.

- Do you need a college degree in order to achieve your career goals?

- To what degree are your parents or guardians involved in discussions about your future?

- Geographically speaking, is it feasible for you to obtain relevant work experience in your field?

- Where can you locate information about volunteer opportunities or job postings in your community?

- If you chose to take a set amount of time away from college academic work to explore career options, how would you support yourself?

- What sensitivities in the environment impact your ability to be successful in an employment setting? How can you find out?

As a college student, it is important to remember that you have access to a number of resources. Many colleges and universities offer counseling services, career planning services, and disability resource centers. As a student with ASD, you might utilize one or all three of these resources at your campus during your career preparation time. The resources do not stop with administrative offices, though. College students often have opportunities to develop their own programming and organizations designed precisely to meet the needs and to address the interests of the student population. If your campus has a library, consider that another resource for you, because during your career exploration, you will likely need to do substantial amounts of research about position openings, professional networks, and business descriptions. Knowing the resources available to you is a responsibility you can maintain by gathering the necessary information in an organized space.

There are a few books listed below, in the Career Preparation Resource Guide, which may aid you during your time in college as you prepare for the next step. Add in other resources at your campus that you may need to access. We have provided several that you may become familiar with during your time at college, but there are likely some that apply specifically to your campus, and there is space for those career preparation resources as well. You may list other books, films, or websites that can help you with career development in your field. When you are struggling to make sense of your future path, recognize that you do not have to, and often should not, feel as though you are alone with some difficult decisions to make. Colleges are designed to educate you and to prepare you for work in society, so their resources will help you through the transitions.

CAREER PREPARATION RESOURCE GUIDE

Resource	Contact	Important Information
Asperger's Syndrome Workplace Survival Guide: A Neurotypical's Secrets for Success	Author, Barbara Bissonnette www.jkp.com	First impressions, communication skills, and executive functions at work
Asperger's on the Job: Must-have Advice for People with Asperger's	Author, Rudy Simone www.fhAutism.com	Real-life scenarios
Disability Resource Center	Director: _____ Website: _____	Accommodations Advocacy Understand ASD
College Career Services	Director: _____ Website: _____	Resume help Practice interviews

LESSON 4: LINKING ACTION AND OPPORTUNITY

Throughout this chapter, you have worked to visually illustrate where you are in terms of your career preparation process, which goals you still need to accomplish, and it is also acknowledged that you might need to take advantage of some resources available during this process. Overwhelming and daunting transition periods, like the one from college to work, can require quite a bit of effort just to maintain an idea of the ultimate goal. When it comes to career discussions, the smaller, detailed steps are difficult to take without some general awareness of big picture purpose. While beginning a lesson broadly can often be challenging for some young adults with ASD, we can use your work in previous lessons to now prepare for managing the details.

Recalling the Career Preparation Puzzle, the purpose of this lesson is to take action to fill any component remaining that you feel is necessary for your career development. For example, if your puzzle lacked pieces for "faculty mentor," "volunteer," and "related work experience," your goal in this lesson is to design a plan to link future employment opportunity with the actions you can take now to fill in the missing puzzle pieces.

What are the pieces from your Career Preparation Puzzle that you have not completed? List the career preparation elements in the box below, and circle the ones you need to make a plan to accomplish.

Missing pieces:

From the example with three remaining pieces—faculty mentor, volunteering, and related work experience—you could gather that a faculty mentor might be the first action step because he or she could be useful in determining where to find volunteer sites and in preparing you for work experience related to the field in which you are both interested. Then, completing some regular volunteer work might be the next step because it may lead to new contacts and related work experience. You may have to prioritize your action steps, and this is sometimes frustrating for students on the spectrum. For many of these prioritizing concerns, you can lay out your options and consider which step would need to happen before all others. Then, you might consider what would reasonably follow that action leading to another, and so on.

Lastly, you will want to set some goals that are associated with real deadlines. Ultimately, you would probably like to have employment options on graduating from college. If that is the final outcome, what your goal is now is to situate the actions that you will have to take before that outcome can occur. You would not likely have, for example, work experience, without also having been interviewed. So, if you have not been interviewed, one step you might plan for with a short deadline is to participate in a mock interview on your campus. After that, you may compile a resume. You can use the deadlines, like mid-term or a holiday break, that your college uses to organize your action plan, or you may choose to intentionally avoid those same deadlines.

In the following activity, focus on prioritizing the action steps that you need to take in order to accomplish your long-term goal. There are a few tips listed that you can use to complete the activity. You will essentially be outlining a series of action steps that you can plan for and take, one at a time, to provide some structure and guidance through your career preparation process and all of its many stages.

TIPS

- List your "big picture" goal first. Refer to it when you have trouble prioritizing.

- Be realistic with your timeline. If you have not compiled a resume, for example, you will not be able to interview for related work experience in one day.

- Feel free to adjust deadline labels. For example, if it is helpful for you to remember "by New Year's Eve" better than the simple "in three weeks" category, label it as such.

- Share your action plan with your mentor or a campus resource person. Ask for feedback about your timeline.

- Be aware that you might need to be flexible with the timing of your action plan. You may volunteer three weeks before your deadline, which would leave room for you to adjust your next action step and complete it sooner, or address another career development goal.

The chapters that follow address many of the pieces you may be missing. Look ahead to consider planning to accomplish an action task that correlates with the supporting activities in the text.

ACTION PLANNING AND MAKING CONNECTIONS

ACTION

- Deadline
- How will you take action?

CAREER

While opportunities certainly can come about randomly, with little or no prior effort on your part, there is a significant chance that if you link your action plan to your big picture goal, you will be prepared for opportunities that do occur randomly, but better yet, you will be able to actively seek them out. Taking proactive steps to increase your marketability while you are a young adult in college can only help you prepare for the possibilities that will be open to you. As a student on the spectrum, you will want to be prepared for the environmental influences on your decisions, for the inevitable need to consult a resource, and for taking manageable action steps toward a greater goal. Structuring your career preparation in a way that complements your academic progress can make a difference in your ability to navigate the demands.

The big picture of success can drive your efforts with career development. Knowing *why* you must take action helps you to frame your career preparation as an imperative rather than an option. Young adults with ASD can prepare for some aspects of the career exploration process that require practice and additional structure by implementing an action plan that outlines their goals. In the next chapter, you will explore some nuances involved in planning for success, like developing a resume and the potential opportunities for networking in your college campus.

BACK TO BASICS

Consider these guiding questions as you prepare to evaluate yourself.

B 1 2 3	**Behavior**	Are you thinking in terms of your big picture plans? Are your actions contributing to your big picture of success? Are you setting goals? Are you asking for clarification throughout this process? Are you practicing flexibility of thought through this transition process?
A 1 2 3	**Academics**	Are you managing your time balancing career exploration and course work? Are you applying organizational strategies? Are your major related courses playing a part in your big picture of success? Do you have a professional mentor on your campus? Are you engaging in opportunities to help you identify your professional niche?
S 1 2 3	**Self-care**	Are you getting enough sleep? Are you eating healthily? Are you planning for your self-care activities? Are you taking time to reflect on your progress? Are you using your time management strategies? Do you feel balanced?
I 1 2 3	**Interaction**	Are you checking in with your support team? Are you expressing interest to others about obtaining an internship? Are you acting on expanding your network? Have you job shadowed someone in a related field? Are you looking for opportunities in your community? Do others see you as motivated? Is your harmonizing role creating a balance?
C 1 2 3	**Community**	Are your environment and the influential people in your life contributing to your journey towards a successful future? Do you feel connected? Are you making connections? Are you utilizing your support team to help you get connected?
S 1 2 3	**Self-monitoring**	Is your energy equally distributed between career search and academics? Are you holding yourself accountable? Are you preparing for upcoming transitions? Are you advocating for yourself? Are you realistic about your expectations?

BACK TO BASICS: RATE YOURSELF

B	**Behavior** 1 2 3	**Comments**
A	**Academics** 1 2 3	**Comments**
S	**Self-care** 1 2 3	**Comments**
I	**Interaction** 1 2 3	**Comments**
C	**Community** 1 2 3	**Comments**
S	**Self-monitoring** 1 2 3	**Comments**

GOALS

Personal:

Academic:

Social:

Chapter 5

REALISTIC CAREER PREPARATION

INTRODUCTION

Students with ASD are presented with many opportunities for development in college, and considering the unique social atmosphere, can benefit from some guidance through the nuances of the shift in focus to include career preparation. As students near the end of their high school days, they will have shifted focus to prepare for college. While daily homework and any extracurricular activities and social life persist, students are also charged with meeting the college preparation demands. Keeping track of application deadlines, writing essays, taking college entrance examinations, and visiting college campuses are all typically happening for high school students as they continue to navigate other more present high school issues like pop quizzes, homecoming, or prom. This kind of overlap in responsibility is also evident in the transition from college to a career. Preparing for these additional career-directed responsibilities beyond academic work in college is a multifaceted and complex process, but much is to be gained from focusing on the small steps that lead to students' career goals.

Since we know that ASD can impact students in many of the areas that are involved in career exploration, there are some strategies to engage students with ASD in a structured, meaningful, and effective career preparation process. In this chapter, the goal is that readers will gain a solid foundational platform of career readiness fundamentals necessary for moving forward in the transition from college to the workplace. Students will need to explore how the transition in their focus while in college will impact all areas of their lives. In addition, students will learn how networking can transform an otherwise confusing social world into one that has specific intention and more clearly defined, if only slightly, social expectations. Reviewing content from Chapter 4, students will construct a resume from their experiences and interests. Finally, in order to have the best chances of success in the career preparation process, students can explore how to realistically increase their marketability while they maintain their academic standing at college.

LESSON 1: EXPLORING THE COLLEGE-TO-CAREER TRANSITION

If you think back to your last two years of high school, you will likely recall the stressful time during your college application process. You had to choose which schools you would apply to, decide how you would manage financially as a college student, complete multiple applications with essays and monotonous forms, even interview for admission in some cases, and all of this occurred while your primary responsibility was being a high school student. Neurotypical students and students with ASD alike who attend college can remember this time as a significant transition period. In many ways, the transition out of college and onto the next step of adulthood is similar to the transition into college. Of course there are differences, and this transition to employment may be more demanding and unfamiliar, but all college students, and especially those with ASD, can benefit from learning about basic fundamental elements to the process during the transition, just as it was necessary to take some essential steps to get into college.

As a college student, you have responsibilities that expend your energy and demand your time. At the very minimum, you have to attend your courses and complete your assignments and exams for each of them. You might also hold membership in various interesting student clubs, regularly attend special campus events, enjoy spending time with your peers in social settings, and carry out a vigorous exercise regime. It can be difficult to imagine adding additional responsibilities to your already demanding schedule as a college student. Yet, just like when you were applying for college, the transition period begins with necessary preparation. As a student with ASD, it is essential that you maintain structure as you begin to integrate new responsibilities.

Your daily responsibilities in college can leave you questioning how it could be possible for you to manipulate your schedule to include career preparation work. Professionals learn quickly in their field that scheduling can make the difference between completing a project and receiving positive feedback from supervisors, and missing important deadlines or appointments. Bosses do not accept excuses regarding this type of mistake, so as an individual with ASD, you will need to take special care to manage your schedule. Generally, the primary responsibility for college students that must be scheduled around would be the academic courses. Most other scheduling, with perhaps the exception of a part-time job or regular volunteer work, is more flexible. Typically, if you are in an organization like an academic club or intramural sports, your time commitment to these extracurricular activities is minimal, and meetings and events often occur once a week after hours. For you, this is a great situation. As you prepare to adjust your schedule to include job preparation, having some flexibility that is afforded by the college experience means you can make the most of your time at college.

When it comes to realistically preparing for schedule changes, you may benefit from viewing a to-do list based on what a professional's schedule may be, day to day (see Figure 5.1). You will notice that this professional has meetings, office work time, and has to make time to complete errands and see friends and family. As a student with

ASD, there may be additional elements you want to consider as you take a look at the example list. You may need to reserve time to pursue your special interests, and include some time to relax. Many professionals schedule personal time for evenings or weekends as their schedule allows. Generally speaking, though, a typical week schedule is full of commitments, and professionals must navigate their responsibilities with structure and flexibility. This list does not include daily tasks that occur each day at a regular time, so all of the tasks must be completed between regular time demands that are not listed. Take a look at the following example of a professional's to-do list for one weekday. Take notes of any thoughts you have in the margins of the page.

MONDAY

- Drop off rent payment at leasing office before 9am
- Go for a run (45 minutes)
- Refill gas tank
- Email J. Scott to follow up on Friday conference call
- Clean office to find O.P. file
- Read newsletter from headquarters
- Type notes from Thursday meeting
- Prepare presentation for tomorrow
- Meet with Bill (take notes from Friday)
- Grocery store and pharmacy on lunch break
- Walk the dog
- Cook dinner and clean up
- Review daily notes from work
- Respond to email RSVP request for Friday's BBQ at Pete's
- Send flowers to mom for birthday

FIGURE 5.1 EXAMPLE OF A TO-DO LIST

Now, using your knowledge about realistic professional scheduling, take some time to work with your own schedule. Considering the example to-do list and all the tasks a professional might keep track of, take a few minutes with your schedule, and find some times that you can dedicate each week to your career exploration efforts. You may find that there are flexible times that you did not expect to have available. Some students may prefer to block off a couple of hours one evening a week to work, and others may want to dedicate 20 minutes more frequently according to a set routine. However you choose to outline your schedule, try your best to adhere to it for at least two weeks.

Then, re-evaluate it and make adjustments as needed. Here are some questions you may consider as you work through this process:

- Do you prefer to sustain effort during a single session, or do you prefer to break work into shorter, more frequent sessions?

- What potential barriers may prevent you from adhering to your schedule?

- Have you considered personal time that you may need in order to work at your best when it is time to work?

- If you travel to a separate area to do career work on your campus, have you considered what this additional time means for your schedule?

- How will you prepare for your work sessions? What will you need with you?

- Are you most alert and focused in the morning, daytime, or night?

- Realistically, how long can you sustain effort before needing to change tasks? Does your schedule reflect this?

- If you are having trouble finding time to work in your existing schedule, are there options for flexibility?

LESSON 2: NETWORKING POTENTIAL

When it comes to career preparation, networking can be a daunting concept for students on the spectrum, but if you embrace it and continue to develop skills to navigate social nuances, the rewards can be bountiful. If you have heard the common phrase, "it's not *what* you know, it's *who* you know," you may be familiar with the idea of networking as a key element in your career progression. When you think about a network, there are many different connections between points, and connections between those points, and so on and so on. These links in a network between set points allow for the exchange of information. In a social context, networking serves to link individuals to others who may share interests, goals, and access to an infinite pool of potential connections. Networking at a fundamental level is simply engaging with others in an intentional way. In order to take advantage of what is perhaps the most influential resource during your career search, you will need to work with other people to reach your goals.

As a college student, you are situated in a uniquely beneficial environment for networking. Between your classmates in each of your classes, your professors, the staff members on your campus, and your friends and family, there are significant opportunities for you to meet people who have the potential to have an impact on your future career path.

Networking does not have to be an intimidating process, and the idea that you can utilize your existing relationships to access opportunities can serve to provide you with a safe network starting point. As you develop a more defined concept of your realistic dream job, which we will explore in more depth later in this chapter, you will learn that your networking efforts will also become more defined by default.

In the boxes below, write down the names of at least five people who initially come to mind when you think about networking, and note your reasoning for each person. Also, be sure to write down their contact information. These five people you have identified can be great resources for you, not only because they are important and trustworthy enough for you to list, but also, since they know you, they will understand how ASD impacts you in social situations, and may offer feedback and guidance as you begin networking.

NETWORKING CONTACTS

Name:

Contact Information:

Name:

Contact Information:

Name:

Contact Information:

Name:

Contact Information:

Name:

Contact Information:

Another person you may want to consider viewing as a networking asset, if you have not already done so, is a mentor in your academic field. A faculty mentor may not only guide you through your academic program and help you consider possibilities in your field, but he or she also likely has many personal connections in the same field. These connections open doors for you to meet new people with the potential to impact your path. For example, if you are working with an instructor who is also a mentor in the business field, she has connections to other instructors who also have significant insight and experience with business. Connecting with these people could lead to career opportunities, and it all began from networking with one person and being open to new people.

Some students with ASD find networking challenging because of the social aspect, but remembering the purpose for your social interactions with people in your field, which is seeking career information and identifying potential career advancement opportunities, the mystery of the conversations is lessened. In the social context of networking, most people are more concerned with meeting people who have something to offer them in terms of their career rather than impressing them with their charm. As you pursue opportunities to practice networking, realize that your everyday interactions are chances for you to present yourself as a marketable potential employee for any number of people you interact with each day.

LESSON 3: RESUME DEVELOPMENT

Networking allows students to meet important people who can influence their future and help them reach their goals, but students with ASD will also need to compile relevant information to provide to potential employers or internship supervisors. When people apply for work, one of the most essential pieces an applicant presents to potential employers is a resume. This is a structured document that illustrates your basic contact information, any previous work history, valuable experiences you have had, education and degrees, and relevant information about you that suggests you would qualify for a particular position. Your resume will typically be the first piece of information a potential employer has about you. It is important that you have this document available throughout your career exploration process as you could need to distribute it quickly as opportunities come about, and waiting until it is too late to compile, draft, and edit your resume could mean you miss out on a valuable work experience. In this lesson, your goal will be, using your puzzle information from Chapter 4 earlier, to create a draft of your resume.

While there is not necessarily a universally used template for the creation of a resume, most need to cover the same or similar sets of information depending on the desired position. The structure and order of items may change from resume to resume, but the general idea stays the same. So one resume may list education before work history, while another may begin with work history and end with education. This may matter more as you work to tailor your resume to specific positions for which you are applying, but if you are just creating a resume, worry less now about order and more about content. You want to be sure that your resume reflects all the effort you have put into obtaining a position, so just focus on establishing a clear and succinct way to present this to potential employers. While people with ASD are all individual and the impact is varied, one commonality is difficulty with the writing process because people with ASD process information differently (Geither and Meeks 2014). This is all the more reason to begin this process early.

To simplify this process, students with ASD may wish to think about information for resumes in three general topics: personal contact information, education history, and work history. First, we can take a look at the way some of the puzzle pieces you worked through in Chapter 4 can help you build your resume in the education and work history areas. As a young adult in college, you will likely have some pieces of your puzzle, including those relevant ones that are listed below, still unfilled. At this point, those left unfilled will simply serve to guide your direction for more growth and skill development. For example, if you do not have the "Related work experience" puzzle piece filled in, then it should be a focus for you going forward. It may help to write a rough draft of your resume in a format designed to help you designate which of your experiences you will want to present. For now, just copy down the information from your puzzle pieces under the resume topics on the next page so you will have some beginning structure for developing your resume.

RESUME TOPIC: EDUCATION HISTORY
RELEVANT PUZZLE PIECES

- "General education requirements"

  _____

- "Campus organizations"

  _____

- "Interest/skills/major"

  _____

- "Academic major"

  _____

- "Earn a degree"

  _____

RESUME TOPIC: WORK HISTORY
RELEVANT PUZZLE PIECES

- "Volunteer"

  _____

- "Work experience"

  _____

- "Related work experience"

  _____

- "Internship"

  _____

The factors you wrote out on the previous page will compose the gist of your resume. More minor elements, though still important, will be crafting descriptions of your duties in any particular role, and outlining a timeline of your experience in each of the topics. Before you begin with these next pieces of the resume, take a look at the example of a student's resume (Figure 5.2, page 94). This student wishes to work as an advocate for the ASD community, so note that many of her resume factors represent her pursuit of this goal. In addition, note the layout and structure of her document. In the activity for this lesson, fill in a template resume designed to mimic this example. Fill it in with information from your puzzle pieces and the descriptions of your effort with the timeline of their occurrence. Remember that not all resumes will necessarily look the same, with the same order of components, but most will need to have the components listed on one page, highlighting the applicant's most marketable career aspects. After you have filled in the template, type your resume, paying attention to the layout of the document, and presenting your information as clearly as possible.

Erin Maynard

1234 West Fairview Drive • Norris, TN, 37890
Home: (615)123-4567
Cell: (615)123-6789
Erin.Maynard@example.com

EDUCATION

University of Tennessee at Chattanooga   **2012–Present**
Bachelor of Science in Psychology   **(Projected Graduation: May 2016)**

EXPERIENCE

MoSAIC Program—Disability Resource Center—U.T. Chattanooga   **2014–Present**
Research Assistant
- Organize progress reports for students in the Mosaic program
- Assist in the development of a resource data base specific to research of Autism Spectrum Disorder
- Maintain confidentiality

W Squared   **June–August 2014**
Information Technology Summer Intern
- Configured computers
  » Installed software (e.g. Microsoft Word, Adobe Flash, Adobe Reader, Adobe Acrobat)
  » Added computers to local domain
  » Backed-up computers to an external drive and transfered information to a new computer
- Assisted in customer services
- Compiled Hardware and Software Inventory

First United Methodist Church Day Camp   **2007–2013**
Camp Counselor for K–4th Grade
- Set up activities
- Organized talent shows
- Supervised children

ACHIEVEMENTS

- Student Representative on Disability Resource Center Advisory Board   2013–Present
- Speaker at 2nd Annual DiversAbility Event at UTC   2014
- Alternate Spring Break participant at UTC   2013
- First United Methodist Church Youth Council   2010–2012
- Model United Nations Conference   2009, 2011

VOLUNTEER EXPEREINCE

- Joe's Storehouse Food Pantry
- Open Table Soup Kitchen
- TEAMeffort Service Organization
- Chattanooga Autism Center
- Chattanooga Autism Awareness Walk

COMPUTER SKILLS

- Proficient with Microsoft Word, Excel, PowerPoint, Access, Internet, Data Collection and Research

*References Available Upon Request

FIGURE 5.2 EXAMPLE OF A STUDENT RESUME

 **BLANK RESUME**

Name: _____
Address _____
_____
Number: _____
Email: _____

EDUCATION

University: _____

Degree: _____

Expected graduation date: _____

University GPA: _____

WORK EXPERIENCE

Company: _____   **Start/End Date of Employment:** _____
Position Title: _____
- Duties: _____
- Duties: _____
- Duties: _____
- Duties: _____

Company: _____   **Start/End Date of Employment:** _____
Position Title: _____
- Duties: _____
- Duties: _____
- Duties: _____
- Duties: _____

Company: _____   **Start/End Date of Employment:** _____
Position Title: _____
- Duties: _____
- Duties: _____
- Duties: _____
- Duties: _____

SKILLS AND CERTIFICATIONS

_____
_____
_____

ACTIVITIES AND HONORS

_____
_____
_____

REFERENCE

Name: _____   **Contact Number:** _____
Position: _____
Name: _____   **Contact Number:** _____
Position: _____

Now that you have a resume to work with, you can start planning for a realistic career path. For many students with ASD, recognizing some of the individual steps toward a long-term goal can be overwhelming, and some students may have difficulty developing realistic ideas for their future career. Your resume will be a document that you work with consistently throughout your career exploration stages. As you become more familiar with your resume, you can add elements to it with your new experiences and tailor its contents to positions as they change. Knowing your own experiences well and understanding how they apply to your goals for the future is essential. Your resume can help you manage and demonstrate your experience in a clear and concise way to employers, and help you clarify and maintain your goals.

CAREER EXPLORATION GUIDE: OPTION TWO

Position Title:

Job Tasks:

Environmental Factors:

Accommodation Needs, if any:

Application and Interview Process:

Education Requirements:

Employment Experience:

Relocation or Travel:

Salary Range:

CAREER EXPLORATION GUIDE: OPTION THREE

Position Title:

Job Tasks:

Environmental Factors:

Accommodation Needs, if any:

Application and Interview Process:

Education Requirements:

Employment Experience:

Relocation or Travel:

Salary Range:

Instead of narrowing your options and your career preparation work to a particular region doing specific work, consider the steps that you may need to take before a giant leap is a reasonable move. Focus on the first step, which will likely be to gain experience in the field while you are still in college in order to prepare for environment changes, and put your effort into developing the skills necessary for a variety of jobs. You have many valuable assets to present to an employer, so be realistic and avoid limiting your growth by narrowing your directions and goals so you can spend more time gaining important career development skills and less time wondering how to make a single opportunity work out.

BACK TO BASICS

Consider these guiding questions as you prepare to evaluate yourself.

B Behavior 1 2 3		Are you engaging in networking opportunities? How are you managing stress? Are you attending appointments and courses and are you prepared and on time? How do you respond to changes in schedule?
A Academics 1 2 3		Are you monitoring your grades? How are you keeping up with assignments and career exploration? Do you know what academic preparation you need for a career? Does your resume reflect your college efforts?
S Self-care 1 2 3		How are you managing daily responsibilities? Are you sleeping and eating enough? Are you maintaining balance? Are you maintaining age-appropriate hygiene?
I Interaction 1 2 3		Are you utilizing professional social skills? Do you value supportive people as you work to reach your goals? Have you identified several potential networking contacts?
C Community 1 2 3		Are you working with an advisor for support? Who can you look to for networking tips? How are your college membership communities supportive?
S Self-monitoring 1 2 3		Are you adhering to a routine? Are you advocating for yourself? Are you engaging professionally with others? Are you considering realistic career options?

⬇ BACK TO BASICS: RATE YOURSELF

B	**Behavior** 1 2 3	**Comments**
A	**Academics** 1 2 3	**Comments**
S	**Self-care** 1 2 3	**Comments**
I	**Interaction** 1 2 3	**Comments**
C	**Community** 1 2 3	**Comments**
S	**Self- monitoring** 1 2 3	**Comments**

GOALS

Personal:

Academic:

Social:

Chapter 6

THE INTERVIEW

INTRODUCTION

The interview process is tantamount to the success or failure of any budding career. Knowing what to say, what to wear, the questions that will be asked, who will be asking the questions, and even where to go is stressful even for neurotypicals, but the process can be horrifying, to say the least, for individuals on the autism spectrum. Interviewing is an inevitable part of life. Interviews are part of every aspect of life, and are the key to obtaining the career you wish. But before an interview can even happen, there are some checkpoints along the way that must be completed.

There are several steps leading up to an interview, and the process itself is very involved and complex. This process requires maximum and sustained effort to be successful. It is important for students to recognize that the more work put in ahead of time, the less stressful and better prepared they will be when opportunities are presented. There are several activities throughout this chapter that will challenge students, all of which are extremely valuable in preparation for not only the interviewing process, but for their work life in general.

Throughout this chapter we highlight parts of the job search and interview process that individuals with ASD commonly share as difficulties. Readers will begin to explore the value in tailoring their resumes according to the position being applied for, and ways to target key words within job descriptions. Throughout this chapter, the self-discovery activities from previous chapters will be revisited as a way to help students thoroughly engage in the activities.

Keep in mind that this chapter only skims the surface of the job searching and interview preparation. We have targeted some basic steps, but encourage all readers to continue independent research and to always remember that the more one invests in this process, the more one will get out of it. College students must have a plethora of support available to them in their respective campuses, such as career placement centers and personal development centers. Those in the community may also have resources available through agencies such as career development centers and the

Department of Vocational Rehabilitation. Participants are encouraged to take an active role in conducting personal research into the community to identify what resources are available to support individuals with ASD through this process. Although they may not have an understanding of the specific needs of an individual on the autism spectrum, they can be very valuable at the start of one's journey.

LESSON 1: SKILL SET AND PREP WORK

There are several ways to go about finding jobs that are available in your area or field of study. Looking for a job can be a difficult process, though, and will take plenty of time and patience. While you may possess the required education and desire to work in the field, this does not necessarily mean that you will get the job you want. As the job market begins to pick up, the challenging task you will most likely face will be the difficult task of finding a job that matches your qualifications, skill set, and interests. This is referred to as "finding your professional niche."

Think back to previous chapters and what you identified as your interests, talents, and skills. It is important to highlight some of these strengths and skill sets as you prepare for the interview process. Use the tools provided in this chapter to help you begin this important process. This is the first step toward your potential career, and every opportunity in which you engage can have a lasting positive effect on your professional career.

The first step in the interview process is to research the company and the job for which you are applying. This information will not only serve as a method of evaluation to determine whether the company or job would be a good fit for you, but in addition, talking about the information you discover during an interview demonstrates enthusiasm about the potential partnership. There are many factors that could make the company a good fit for a candidate, and many can be revealed through an analysis of the company's website. The company's mission statement, vision statement, images on the website, or highlighted documents speak clearly of its values. If the highlighted values match your personal core values, you can establish a goodness of fit with the company and you can share that information through your covering letter introducing yourself, resume, and interview.

During the job search process, you will likely interview for several jobs at various companies, so keeping all the information organized is vital. When you speak about a company's mission, be confident that you are speaking about the correct company. When you talk about the initiatives being pursued, it is imperative that you talk about the correct information. Discussing inaccurate information or information about the wrong company can very quickly become a road block in this process. Below is a useful tool to help guide you through the research prior to actually securing an interview. For each job posting or lead that interests you, take the time to think about the items listed in the brainstorming sheet provided.

PRIOR TO SUBMITTING YOUR RESUME OR APPLICATION

Job applied for: _____

Interesting facts about the company:

    1. _____

    2. _____

    3. _____

Interesting facts about the company's history:

    1. _____

    2. _____

    3. _____

Is this a reputable job? Yes / No

Skills that qualify you for this position: _____

_____

Key words in the job description that stand out to you: _____

_____

What about your degree/experiences align with what they are looking for?

_____

_____

What about the company's mission/vision statements align with your values?

_____

_____

When was this position posted: _____

The deadline for submitting your application/resume: _____

Concerns: _____

_____

_____

If you are invited for an interview, it means that you have the required skills and experience the company is looking for (Bissonnette 2012). But this does not mean that every job you apply for, or qualify for, will invite you for an interview. Do not let this discourage you along the way. An average person can submit in the range of 30 resumes for jobs, but may only be called in for three interviews. The pool of applicants typically is large, which is why it is so important to have a positive interview. Most people are hired for a job because they have made a connection with someone on the interviewing team. While neurotypicals depend on and place value on interpersonal connections during the interview process, individuals on the spectrum tend to focus on academic success, definitive skill sets, and work environment preferences, as these are areas that they consider important. This distinction can be very frustrating for people with ASD because the connection may not be established and the job could be offered to another applicant, although the person with ASD is as, if not more, qualified. However difficult to accept, this is the reality. During the interview, employers are not only looking for the most qualified person, but also for goodness of fit, and will seek out the person who will mesh well with their existing team.

Although it is not a natural strength, there are methods people with ASD can take to make connections. This links directly back with researching the company, expectations, and leadership of the company. Identify areas that you also relate to, and prepare and rehearse some talking points prior to entering the interview. Another good approach to forming interpersonal connections with the interviewer is to approach the interview with enthusiasm. This will demonstrate that you are invested and want to work with them; do not try to feign enthusiasm, however, or be overly enthusiastic. It is easy to tell when people are faking enthusiasm, and this will turn an interview panel off very quickly. Practice interview skills and have someone give you feedback about your level of engagement and enthusiasm. Adjust your responses accordingly, and practice again so that when you take part in an actual interview, it will potentially be a more comfortable experience.

Finally, as you prepare for the interview process, it is imperative that you know as much as possible about the job for which you are applying. You can practice interview responses, but know that your responses are expected to be adjusted according to the expectations of the position. Be mindful of how your responses represent you and your qualification, as well as how they match the expectations of the position. It may seem that there is a lot of work and details to consider in preparation for an interview, but the more work you put into the preparation, the better opportunity for a successful interview. The more committed you are to the prep work, the more committed you will be in the interview, and this will be evident to a potential employer.

The interview process is inevitably more difficult for people with ASD, but it is the necessary first step to beginning a career. To begin your prep work, review the following sample responses and spend time drafting some of your own responses. Again, your responses will need to be tailored for each interview, but these responses can be used for your practice interviews.

INTERVIEW PRACTICE RESPONSES

Question: Tell me a little bit about yourself.

Example response: Well, I am a junior at the University of Tennessee at Chattanooga majoring in mechanical engineering. I have a strong desire to work hard and excel at everything I do. I really enjoy learning new things and investing in things that interest me. I am an eagle scout and have learned a great deal of leadership skills through my experience and community service over the years. I would consider myself detail-oriented and someone who follows directions well. I ran across this job opportunity while checking my email last week. I read the description and felt like this was exactly what I was looking for in an internship. I am really looking for an opportunity to apply the knowledge and skills I have learned in the classroom to the real world.

Your response:

_____

_____

_____

_____

_____

_____

Question: What would you identify as some of your strengths?

Example response: I am really strong academically, so I would say some of my strengths would be that I am punctual with deadlines, detail-oriented, decent at analyzing data, and always on time. I see a need and I am able to get things done for the most part, of course with a learning curve. A lot of my more recent projects have been group projects and although I prefer to work alone, lately I have noticed the leadership role I take on, and have enjoyed working in groups. I think group work has allowed me the opportunity to recognize areas in which I have competency, but also how those fit into the atmosphere of a team.

Your response:

_____

_____

_____

_____

_____

Question: What would you identify as some of your weaknesses?

Example response: You know, if you had asked me that question a few years ago I might have answered by saying "my passion" is my weakness. I really invest in the work that I do, but within the last year or so I have learned how to invest my time and energy more effectively. Right now I would say one of my biggest challenges is that I focus a lot on over-thinking details of a task. Mainly I think this is because I am always looking for ways to improve and implement best practice. I think sometimes being detail-oriented has its advantages, but can present its own challenges too.

Your response:

_____

_____

_____

_____

_____

Questions: If you got frustrated with a co-worker, whether it be a boss or colleague, how would you handle the situation?

Example response: This has always been a hard one for me. I would first go to the co-worker and let them know what was frustrating me. I would ask for clarification before I let myself get too frustrated. Honestly, I would do my best to see if we could resolve the issue ourselves. I think part of being an effective team member is not only being qualified for a position, but also someone who gets along with others. Sometimes that means learning when to step away from the situation in the moment of frustration and accepting others' differences. I would do my best not to discuss the issue with other team members, and if necessary I would report to my immediate supervisor for guidance. I think it is important to recognize we spend more time at work than we do at home, so getting along, regardless of our differences, is very important to me.

Your response:

_____

_____

_____

_____

_____

_____

Questions: Where do you see yourself in five years' time?

Example response: To be honest, I don't know if I can answer that. I am more of a here-and-now thinker, so who knows what will happen over the next five years. Ideally I would like to see myself somewhere in this company, serving both customers and working towards the company's objectives. My hope is that I will be in a stable job and enjoying what I do while making a positive impact on my community. I will be honest and say I will be where opportunity is. I believe and will invest in a position in which I have the opportunity to grow and develop not only professionally, but also personally. I think if someone is not in a place where they are experiencing growth, they are not really where they need to be. I want to be challenged and put outside of my comfort zone, not stagnate and be comfortable.

Your response:

_____

_____

_____

_____

_____

_____

Question: Do you have any questions for us?

Example response: Yes, actually I do. We have talked a lot about me, but I am really interested in what you are looking for in a mechanical engineer intern. What would a day in this position look like? Can you tell me about the team I would be working with? What are the next steps in this process?

Your response:

_____

_____

_____

_____

_____

_____

As you develop your own responses to these standard interview questions, practice the responses with a person who will give you honest feedback. Video your practice interview sessions, and adjust your responses and enthusiasm to be more engaging and enthusiastic while staying authentic. This practice and effort will only positively impact your potential for a successful interview, which can then, in turn, set up a good transition into your career.

LESSON 2: VERBAL AND NONVERBAL BEHAVIOR

During the interview process you should be prepared and confident to present yourself as a competent professional, both verbally and nonverbally. By practicing your potential responses to frequently asked interview questions, you will develop more confidence in your ability to express yourself through verbal interactions. The messages sent through verbal interactions, however, are not the only pathway for sending messages. Nonverbal communication happens anytime a person interacts with another person. This message can be intentional or unintentional, but could have a significant impact on the perception of the message (Gabbott and Hogg 2000). Individuals with ASD tend to have some difficulty with both presenting and interpreting nonverbal messages accurately, but with preparation and practice, the impact of this potential barrier can be lessened.

PLANNING PROCESS

- Be on time: You should arrive at the interview location at least 15 minutes before your appointment. This will allow time for unforeseen events such as traffic, weather issues, forgotten items, etc. This will also give you time to get settled into the environment before you come face to face with the interviewer, which is important for making a positive first impression. If you are late for an interview, you will appear to have a poor work ethic, and the interviewer may choose to not hire you before you even begin.

- Know where you going: While setting up the interview, take some time to get clear instructions on where you will need to be on the day of the interview. Large companies and unfamiliar environments are sometimes hard to navigate, especially when you are nervous. A good time to ask for clarification regarding where your interview will take place is during the initial set-up process. If appropriate and possible, it might be a good idea to actually visit the site prior to the interview. This is a way you can explore parking options, and know exactly what your environment will look like.

- Review the job description—know the job and the company: Sometimes people apply for multiple jobs at a time. A good way to prepare for some of the interview questions is to review the job description; sometimes these can have specific details about the job, and can always serve as a refresher for why you were actually initially interested in the position. Sometimes it is also good practice to research the company. This may not only be very informative, but will also show the interviewers that you prepared and care about the position. Maybe one of your strengths is research (if so, try to limit the interesting facts to three to four during the actual interview).

- Identify the person leading the interview, or a point person if possible: Most of the time the person who telephones you is the administrative assistant or a person from human resources. The purpose behind identifying a point person is to know the name and number of someone to call in case an emergency arises. This will also give you a familiar name to remember on the day of the interview.

Use the outline below to help guide you through gathering this information.

SCHEDULING AN INTERVIEW

Job applied for: _____

Who you are speaking with: _____

What date you are scheduling your interview on: _____

Time: _____

With: _____

Where: _____

Directions: _____

_____

_____

Contact number, Point person or Email: _____

BE PROFESSIONAL

- Look the part: The interviewer's first impression of you will be based on your appearance. Your hair should be clean and combed, teeth brushed, and your clothes should be clean and ironed. Men should have a nicely trimmed beard or shave before an interview. It is not mandatory, but it is a good idea to get a haircut a few days before the interview. For women, if you wear make-up, be sure it looks professional. Being mindful of your appearance will make a good impression on the interviewer. Most of the time it is appropriate for you to carry a legal pad or a portfolio. You should have a few copies of your resume and a list of questions in the portfolio.

- Dress the part: Professional attire means different things for different people, and proper attire is different for different professions. If possible, you may want to do a walk-through prior to the interview so you can observe what people are wearing. A safe bet is always to wear business-style casual clothing. Buy your interview clothing early, so that you will feel comfortable in it by the time of the interview. You should also limit the amount of jewelry and perfume/cologne you wear, as you do not want to take attention away from your responses to the questions, or leave a bad impression. Dress today for the job you want tomorrow.

- Be confident: Most people don't actually feel confident in interviews, but it is important to present yourself as confident. This means you should sit up straight, speak clearly, and try to make eye contact. For individuals with ASD, it is important to remember to share the conversation and to make sure to answer the questions asked appropriately. Do your best not to talk in circles, and stay focused. We encourage students to practice answering interviewing questions as often as possible.

- Go in prepared: Do your homework about the company. If you know what the company's mission is, what the company values, how the company started, or any other identifying information about the company, you can talk about that in the interview. This will show the potential employer that you are invested in them. In addition, there are many general questions that most employers ask interviewees. Think about possible questions that may be asked and practice your responses with someone who will give you honest feedback. Possibly video yourself giving responses, or practice answering questions in front of a mirror, and pay close attention to your nonverbals (facial expressions, eye contact, and expressions).

- Invest in yourself: By this we mean show the interviewer that you are interested in the interview process. Be mindful of your posture, responses, and how you market yourself as a professional.

THINGS TO REMEMBER

- Introduce yourself: Introducing yourself seems like a simple task, but when you are nervous, the simplest tasks are the ones we forget. Be sure to introduce yourself, shake hands if necessary, and make eye contact when interacting with the interviewers. Give a warm greeting such as, "Hello, nice to meet you. My name is Molly." If you are being interviewed by one person, you could break the ice by complimenting their office or a piece of art you see on the way to their office. Avoid complimenting people directly, however; this is the first impression you are creating, and if you use the wrong word because you are nervous, this could have a negative impact if directed at the interviewer personally. If you are being interviewed by a group, be sure to introduce yourself and acknowledge each person in the room. You want to establish a positive beginning, so act excited to be there, smile, and make eye contact. Be confident.

- Let the interview guide you: Pay close attention and be aware of the social cues from the people who are interviewing you. Typically you will show up for an interview (15 minutes early) and be asked to wait in the lobby or a conference room. Use this time to settle in, take a few deep breaths and relax. When you are asked to come back or others enter the room, stand up to greet them. This shows them respect. After they introduce themselves, you will want to introduce yourself. If they extend their hand for a handshake, shake their hand. Chances are that they are looking at you when talking to you, so be sure to make eye contact. If eye contact is difficult for you, as it usually is for people with ASD, practice looking at people in the area between the eyes and where the bridge of the nose meets. Too low or too high or no eye contact could have a negative impact on how others perceive you. When they sit down, follow their lead. Most of the time you will be sitting across a desk or around a conference table. Observe the dynamics of the group. If the group is relaxed, you should be relaxed. When being asked questions, be sure to make eye contact and be interactive with the person or the group. A few head nods and a smile show that you are interested and approachable, something they will be looking for. Use the following checklist to help you be prepared for your interview.

PROFESSIONAL INTERVIEW

What to wear: _____
(Remember clean clothes, ironed and appropriate attire)

Grooming Checklist

☐ Hair cut and styled to look professional   ☐ Showered

☐ Facial hair trimmed or shaved, if applicable   ☐ Make-up, if used, is appropriate and professional

☐ Teeth brushed

Ways to feel confident: _____

_____

_____

Dates to remember: _____

_____

FOLLOW UP

- Thank you letter: It is always a good idea to follow up immediately after an interview with a thank you letter or email. In the thank you follow up there are four main points that are important to cover. Format and address the letter or email appropriately, and thank all of those involved for taking the time to meet with you. Next you should remind them of the position you interviewed for, and the date on which the interview occurred. It is always a good idea to briefly reference the skills and experience you have as they relate to the job. Lastly, express your continued interest in the position. Take a look at the sample letter provided below. Use this as a reference and create your own thank you letter.

Molly Ruth
123 Addison Avenue
Chattanooga TN, 37011
TEL: (423)-445-6789

Autism in College, LLC
1234 Aiden Lane
Hixson, TN 083191   July 2, 2016

Dear Search Committee,
Thank you so much for taking the time to meet with on June 30, 2016 regarding the positon as Program Coordinator for Autism in College, LLC. I not only appreciate your time but enjoyed interacting with the team. The team dynamic described during the interview and displayed by the interactions of the committee is exactly what I am looking for. After hearing the needs of your program and the expectation of the Program Coordinator, I feel as if I have the experience and passion that would be an asset to the team. I am eager to take the next steps and will plan to follow up within the next few days to see how the search is going. Please do not hesitate to contact me if you have any future questions. Thank you again for your time and consideration. I look forward to speaking with you in the near future.

Sincerely,
Molly Ruth

FIGURE 6.1 EXAMPLE OF A FOLLOW-UP LETTER

LESSON 3: TO DISCLOSE OR NOT TO DISCLOSE

The decision to disclose to a potential employer is a personal decision and one that must be approached with care and diligence. This decision is a grey area in the process of the job search and interview process that must be analyzed thoroughly before an individual makes a decision. As explored in *Developing Identity, Strengths, and Self-Perception for Young Adults with Autism Spectrum Disorder: The BASICS College Curriculum* (Rigler, Rutherford, and Quinn 2015), the grey area is a particular challenge faced by many individuals with ASD. The decision to disclose the impact of a disability is not right or wrong, black or white, but exists within this grey area. It is important to recognize that life experiences impact the decisions we make, but also allow for opportunity and growth. Some advantages of disclosure are that it could open the door for several opportunities and understanding, and allow for employees to receive the necessary accommodations. To help guide you in your decision-making process, the information in this lesson is offered in three distinct areas: (1) **Why** disclose; (2) **When** to disclose; and (3) **How** to disclose if that is the decision you make.

WHY

In college, in order to receive any academic accommodations to counter the impact of having ASD, students disclose their disability and request accommodations through their college's disability services office. These accommodations allow students to navigate their work and environment at college with the same chance of success as any other neurotypical student. For many, this step of disclosing ASD in college is an important one as the student adjusts to independent life on a college campus. Without disclosing ASD to the appropriate college resources, students do not receive accommodations to counter the impact of having ASD in the classroom and on campus. It is the act of telling the appropriate people on campus that you have ASD that opens up the possibility of those accommodations. In the workplace, just as in college, disclosing ASD to the appropriate person and seeking reasonable accommodations is up to the individual.

If you choose not to disclose that you have ASD, be aware that people involved with any problems that might occur at work or during an interview will have no frame of reference for behaviors they may view as abnormal. Some of these behaviors may include, but are not limited to, stimming because you are nervous, poor eye contact, a shaky voice, or the need for clarification or for a more structured interview. Disclosing does not prevent judgment from co-workers, but it can help explain certain behaviors. If you do not tell your employers about your ASD, it may be difficult to advocate for yourself in terms of accommodations needed at work. It is certainly your own decision regarding whether or not you explain that you have ASD to your employer, and many choose not to disclose, but it is important to understand that support is not required to be provided retroactively. This means that if you are hired for a job, fail to disclose, and then ask for accommodations, and do not perform at the level expected by your employer and are then fired, you cannot then explain that you have ASD and that you needed an accommodation in order to perform as necessary and expect to receive your job back. If, however, you disclose that you have ASD when hired in order to request a specific accommodation or to explain a certain characteristic that might be displayed, then your employer might have more information from which to work off when considering your work performance. Many employers are getting much more proficient at viewing their employees individually with less regard to the costs of accommodations (Meyer 2001).

WHEN

There are a few options for appropriate times to disclose ASD. Some people choose to disclose before the interview. This might be helpful for someone who needs support during the interview itself. Perhaps you would like a chance to see the interview questions the day before the interview so that you have a chance to read, process, and understand them before having to answer them on the spot, in person. Employers are unlikely to consider this request unless there is a legitimate reason. Here, disclosing before the interview can help the employer help you by what can be referred to as leveling the playing field for your potential success. Disclosing before the interview would also be a good option for someone who struggles significantly with communication or displays behavior often perceived as abnormal. You may not need an accommodation for your work environment, but a little explanation can go a long way when it comes to social norms and behavior.

Another option for an appropriate time to disclose is during the interview. This option allows you to explain ASD from your point of view, and what that may mean for your employer. There are several reasons why an employer would want to hire someone with ASD, and disclosing in the interview can give you a chance to explain which of those reasons apply to you. Disclosing in the interview is a way to discuss your strengths in a positive way. It may also be a good time to disclose if you know there will be additional interviews for which you might need support.

You may also choose to disclose ASD when you have been hired. This is an option for those individuals who do not need support during the interview process, but who might need some on-the-job support. Some people choose this option as a way to avoid the stigma associated with ASD while the employer is still making a decision as to whether or not to hire them. Once you have been hired, you can disclose knowing that your job is safe from any judgment by those who do not understand ASD. At this point, the company has seen your strengths, invested in you as a new employee, and will possibly see you as an asset to the team. Sometimes people never officially disclose ASD with their employers, but rather just explain ASD and their experience with it on a personal one-on-one level with co-workers. Others just wait to disclose until there is an issue with the way things are going.

HOW

Depending on when you want to disclose, there are some steps you can take to make the process go smoothly. First, it is important to work with the hiring department or managers. You will want to be sure that the information goes directly to whoever will be interviewing you, and whoever is responsible for making decisions about who is hired. If you make it through the interview process and you are hired, you can meet with your supervisor or representatives from the human resources department where you work to discuss any necessary accommodations.

If you choose to disclose during the interview, it is important to remember social cues and to wait for an appropriate time in the conversation to discuss it. Almost always, at the close of every interview, the interviewee has a chance to ask questions. This is a great time to discuss ASD. You can frame your disclosure into a question, like "What kind of support would be available to me as someone who has ASD?" From there, you can gauge the interviewers' responses, and decide if you want to spend more time explaining ASD to them at that point, or if you want to wait to see if you are hired or until after the hiring process is complete. You may also want to disclose at the beginning of the interview if you want to explain any behavior you feel may interfere with your ability to successfully answer any questions they have for you.

If you disclose when you have been hired, typically the best and most confidential way to disclose is to speak with someone from the human resources department and/or your supervisor. This will ensure that you have an opportunity to request any support or accommodations that will allow you to do your job. You can also discuss having ASD with any of your co-workers at any time you want. At times it may be important to mention ASD if your co-workers do not seem to understand your behavior, or if you are working together on a project and you need to ask for help from one of your group members.

Despite the context within which you disclose, it can help to have a script prepared ahead of time that you can refer to during this conversation. A script can help you practice and remember important points that you need to be sure to explain. In addition to a script, you might consider providing your employer with a list of common ASD traits. The following can be used as a template for your own disclosure script.

"Ms. Sharp, I enjoy working here and I am doing my best to perform well. At times I may be [overwhelmed, confused, speaking too loudly, etc.] and want to offer an explanation to you about my behavior. I have Autism Spectrum Disorder [Asperger's, Autism, ASD] and sometimes I do not understand [social cues] and I have trouble [getting started with really large tasks]. It would be helpful to me if I could [move to a quiet workspace, see an example, work while wearing headphones, etc.]. I would be happy to talk to you about ASD and how it impacts me should you have any questions."

WHAT WOULD YOU DO?

For this exercise, review these cases, choose one and come up with an action plan about how or if that person should disclose ASD at their workplace. Use the space after the examples to document your responses.

Example 1: Simon, a college senior, is applying for a job as an accountant at a local nonprofit agency. He is a great candidate on paper—4.0 GPA [grade point average], recipient of an academic scholarship, and a leader in a college organization for accountants. Simon has ASD and struggles greatly with the interview process, and this has prevented him from obtaining two of the internships he has applied for recently. He has difficulty maintaining eye contact, and is frustrated by misunderstanding the lengthy interview questions. He knows that he would do better if he could receive accommodations during the interview process, but does not know whether or not to disclose that he has ASD.

Example 2: Kendra was hired by her first choice employer on graduating from college. She was hired as part of a manager training program that will provide her with the necessary skills and experience to lead a local branch of the corporation. Kendra did not disclose ASD during the interview process. Now that she has accepted the position, she is considering disclosing to her colleagues. Sometimes Kendra struggles with some of the social norms in the workplace, and she thinks explaining ASD and her perspective as a person on the spectrum will provide some insight on the minor communication challenges she has at work.

Example 3: Martin, a recently graduated architect, who disclosed to his direct supervisor when he accepted his job, has been having some problems at his job. Martin did not ask for accommodations when he began working. Now that he has settled into his job, he is struggling with the environment in which he is expected to work. His desk is beside the entrance to the architecture firm, so he is constantly distracted by people coming and going. He can hear the phone ringing all day and his co-workers shouting from across the room to get feedback on projects or to discuss weekend plans while Martin tries to work. The environment is preventing Martin from doing his best work at a new job, but he doesn't know if it's appropriate to ask for a different work area because of his sensory issues.

Chosen example: _____

Response:

_____

_____

_____

_____

_____

_____

_____

_____

_____

_____

_____

_____

_____

_____

BACK TO BASICS

Consider these guiding questions as you prepare to evaluate yourself.

B　1 2 3	**Behavior**	Are you practicing for interviews? How do you receive feedback from interview behavior? Have you prepared materials for the interview? Do you know where to go and with whom to speak?
A　1 2 3	**Academics**	Are you able to discuss your academic strengths? Do you feel in control of your assignments? Have you researched the academic requirements for the job?
S　1 2 3	**Self-care**	How is your hygiene maintained? Do you know what you will wear to an interview? Are you sleeping and eating enough?
I　1 2 3	**Interaction**	Are you confident in your first impression at an interview? How will you handle social confusion? Are you being polite? Do you listen and value professionals with whom you speak?
C　1 2 3	**Community**	Are you using interview resources on campus? Do you engage with your network? Before and after an interview, are you receiving trusted feedback? Where is your professional niche?
S　1 2 3	**Self-monitoring**	Are you managing your volume and tone of voice during the interview? Have you prepared for possible outcomes? Are you advocating for yourself? Are you maintaining organization?

BACK TO BASICS: RATE YOURSELF

B	**Behavior** 1 2 3	**Comments**
A	**Academics** 1 2 3	**Comments**
S	**Self-care** 1 2 3	**Comments**
I	**Interaction** 1 2 3	**Comments**
C	**Community** 1 2 3	**Comments**
S	**Self-monitoring** 1 2 3	**Comments**

GOALS

Personal:

Academic:

Social:

Chapter 7

WORK EXPOSURE

INTRODUCTION

As college students, young adults focus heavily on the academic demands assigned by professors, but typically spend too little time developing the skills to be able to reach the next goal in their lives. All too often, college students work diligently to choose the right major, read what is assigned, complete the assigned homework, pass exams, etc. all to reach the goal of graduating with a college degree. However, these same students do little work to expose themselves to the world of work. In our recent history, the college graduate was considered a highly sought-after person and was often able to enter a career with ease. Because more students are now graduating and entering the workforce (Green 2013) than before, students must also do some focused work to develop themselves into a well-qualified applicant who can stand out against other applicants.

Young adults with ASD tend to have a more difficult time entering a gainful career than their neurotypical peers (Walsh *et al.* 2014) due to these extra requirements. Because college students with ASD are comfortable focusing on the academics within their chosen majors, the necessary work exposure activities that can help build their qualifications are overlooked because they require becoming familiar with what are often new social and professional territories. These activities tend to be social in nature and require planning, organization, initiation, and good communication, so it is vital for students with ASD to understand the importance prior to engaging in the development process. As with anything, if there is a well-understood purpose and the value is clear, an individual is more likely to engage in this work exposure process.

There are several benefits for starting this process in the middle of a college career, and each of these benefits can be viewed as a potential step for further career success. At the mid-point of the college process, students have typically completed many general education requirements and are becoming settled on a major choice. Students often begin working on major courses and change the focus from college classes to potential careers.

By engaging in this process early, students will primarily gain a better understanding of their career choice. By participating in things like job shadowing or informational interviews, students can develop a concrete understanding of what the experience of their future career may resemble. If the students enjoy the experience and like what they learn, this increased understanding could be the caveat for fully committing to the major choice and career pursuit. Conversely, if they do not enjoy the experience, and the career is something different than expected, this understanding could lead to exploring options for different majors. This increased understanding would serve as a way to discover and develop goodness of fit within the career choice.

By furthering the exposure to a potential career by engaging in formal activities like career fairs or professional networking, a student could gather a bank of highly qualified professionals who could serve as mentors and guides during this exciting time. College students with ASD could benefit greatly from this guidance as they begin to change the goal from graduation to career entry. These experiences can give students a true understanding of what the expectations will be like to enter the workforce. A college degree is not the key to entering the chosen career; instead, it is all the other experiences that come along as students explore the world of work.

LESSON 1: JOB SHADOWING

The experience of job shadowing can be compared to trying on clothes before buying them. As a college student, you have many options ahead of you, but before you commit to your career choice, you should "try it on." Job shadowing allows you to do just that. Although you may have always dreamed of becoming a field geologist, you may realize after a short time that you do not actually like working outside in the elements all the time. This discovery would be better to make prior to graduating with a Geology degree and entering the workforce. If you spend a week shadowing a professional in the field, and spend quality time thoroughly observing the professional, and documenting your observations, you can develop a solid understanding of what the expectations of that career truly are. Students can hear about what to expect from professors and others in the field, but will develop a much broader understanding by shadowing someone and experiencing the work first hand.

The first step in setting up the job shadowing experience is to identify locations in your community that may have professionals working in your chosen career. If you are in a small community, you may need to find a professional with a similar career path that may have some variation from your career goal. This will still give you an indication of the potential day-to-day operations of the career, but may have some variation in the end product. You can gather this information by visiting the career center at your college or possibly reaching out to the Department of Vocational Rehabilitation in your community. As a student, you also have a large network of alumni who are often willing to help a current student, and by contacting the Department of Alumni Affairs you could have access to these professionals as well.

Once you have identified the locations within the community that have professionals employed in your chosen career, the next step is to research the companies so you are knowledgeable about the company's mission and vision. This will help guide you as you make the first contact with the professional you hope to shadow. Examine the company's website, research the organizational structure of the company, identify what the company celebrates as accomplishments, and document the goals and success indicators outlined by its leadership. This information can be used in your initial contact with the person you hope to shadow. Because people are typically very busy in their jobs, having a college student follow them around while they are working may be a difficult sell, but if you do your homework first, they will potentially take you more seriously and see you as a committed pre-professional.

One you have gathered this essential information, you will need to make the first contact with the professional. This initial contact should be in email form so you can present yourself well. Pair the information you found on the website with your own career goals as to why you would like to have this experience with the company, and clearly define what you would like to gain from a job shadow. Finally, identify the timeframe you would like to shadow the professional, and clarify your purpose. Send emails to many professionals in the community to have a better chance of making a match.

Develop a list of things you hope to discover as you research your potential career through job shadowing. These pieces of information could vary from work environment to team dynamics, but will be important to have ahead of time. As an individual with ASD, you are the only one who can know what work environment will lend itself to the most success for you in your career. This is the time to clearly identify those parameters so you can ensure that the career you are planning for will be a good fit for you. Use a notebook and write down these specific parameters so you can be sure to observe them in the field. In this same notebook, outline any specific questions you may have for the professional at the end of your experience. These should be specific to the career at that company, not questions that can be answered by researching careers on the internet. For example, you may want to understand the level of teamwork required in the career. This is something that the professional could answer for you, but you may not be able to find that information easily yourself. Conversely, you could find information about degree requirements or salary potential, so this is not the line of questions you should prepare for your job shadowing experience.

Once you have identified the company and professional who will allow you to shadow them for the timeframe you have outlined, be prepared to also be professional during that time. Dress in clothing that is acceptable in the company, have all of your materials with you including your notebook and/or a small recorder, arrive five minutes early so you can be prepared, and be respectful of the time the professional is giving you. Be willing to ask questions during your time, but do not bombard the person with so many questions that he or she cannot get work completed. Observe everything, and document it in your notebook or with your recorder. Identify the technology used, the tools the person you are shadowing uses during the day, how the person communicates with others in the company, what the level of formality is in the company, etc. Arrive expecting to be a silent observer, but be willing to take part in conversations and meetings as the opportunity arises. The more exposure you have to the work, the more you will be educated about the career and can determine goodness of fit.

As your experience comes to an end, be sure to again be thankful to the professional you shadowed. Acknowledge that he or she has allowed you to be part of their work life for a time, and that the experience has done a great deal to help you as you develop your career path. Take some time to ask any last-minute questions and to allow for the professional to give you last-minute advice. If the experience goes well, this person can become a part of your professional network and can serve as a mentor in the future, so be sure to ask for a business card as you leave. As you conclude this experience, be sure to send an email to the professional you job shadowed to again, thank them for their time and education, and ask them to keep you in mind for future partnerships. This follow-up could leave a lasting impression and could open up potential internships for you in the future.

The Job Shadowing Preparation Guide that follows can help you organize your experience. Use it to prepare your questions and other details you will need so you do not arrive at your job shadowing placement unprepared and make a poor impression.

JOB SHADOWING PREPARATION GUIDE

Potential career:
Community connections:
Career center contacts:
Department of Vocational Rehabilitation contacts:
Alumni Affairs contacts:
Researched information about the company:
Scripted introductory email:
Potential discoveries:
Potential questions:
Advice offered:
Follow-up scripted email:

LESSON 2: INFORMATIONAL INTERVIEWS

Informational interviews are another way to learn about your potential careers, but they are also a way to make connections within the field, and to build your professional network. A well-designed informational interview could not only allow a person with ASD to learn a great deal about a company and a career, but can also serve as a way for professionals in the field to get to know the person and his or her particular skill set in a nonthreatening way. By engaging in this pre-professional activity, you could make lasting connections with potential employers as you complete your college career.

Informational interviews differ greatly from interviews for a specific position. Career seekers, for the purpose of gathering vital information about a potential career or career change, initiate informational interviews. These conversations are not about gaining employment for a specific position, but about gathering data about a potential career path or company. While the focus is specifically on gathering information from the person being interviewed, this is also a time to gather intelligence about sought-after skills within the field to help you become gainfully employed in the future.

As you plan for your informational interview, you should consider the information that will solidify your decision in your chosen career path. The typical direction of these conversations usually includes questions regarding the preferred college degree and experience, the career trajectory within the field, and the future trends within the field. However, as a person with ASD, it may also be vital for you to consider the work environment within the company (open concept work spaces or private work spaces), the respected soft skills within the company (social gatherings as an expectation, collaborative working teams, etc.), and the possibility of a career mentor. Designing your informational interview into these two distinct sections can serve as a reminder that each section is important and necessary as you explore your career options.

Another thing to consider as you enter your career search is that every person with whom you come into contact during the informational interview phase could potentially become a member of your professional network. Although this is not a formal interview, this could be a time to highlight some of your experiences and skills. Through this process, the person with whom you are meeting could see something valuable in you as a potential future employee within the company. This person could refer you to another professional who could have some impact on your future career. You may have the possibility of an internship, apprenticeship, or a professional mentorship as a result of this brief meeting.

Because of the potential impact of this meeting, it is vital that you carry yourself professionally and respectfully. Acknowledge that the person you met with has taken the time out of his or her day to help you understand your potential career choice, shake hands, and ask for a business card to add to your collection of professional contacts. As with any meeting, it is important to follow up the meeting with a genuine thank you email to the person with whom you met. This will leave a lasting effect on them of the meeting with you, and can serve as a catalyst for the person to want to engage you in further conversations. The next page offers a structured space for your notes from informational interviews.

INFORMATIONAL INTERVIEW STRUCTURE

Business card information

Name:_____   Email:_____

CAREER TRAJECTORY QUESTIONS

*What is the preferred college degree?

*What is the potential career growth?

*What are some potential future trends for the field?

CAREER TRAJECTORY QUESTIONS

*What is the physical working environment like?

*What are the social expectations at this company?

*What is the potential for a career mentor?

⬇ INFORMATIONAL INTERVIEW REFLECTIONS

_____

_____

_____

_____

_____

_____

Thank you email date sent: _____   Response received: _____

LESSON 3: CAREER FAIRS

Many colleges and universities offer career fairs each year. Most colleges offer general career fairs as well as field-specific career fairs. These events are offered to allow companies to set up and meet future graduates from the college. This is often the first exposure many future graduates have to potential employers, and a company's first exposure to potential employees. It is common for nearly 100 companies to set up tables next to each other in a large meeting room, which could lead to sensory overload for students with ASD. The representatives will be prepared to share information about their respective companies, offer information in paper form, accept resumes, and will occasionally conduct initial interviews if they are impressed with a resume.

This initial exposure to potential employers is incredibly important in the career search. This is how many future graduates gain the first round of interviews for the partnership companies. Companies that attend the college career fairs often have a relationship with the college and purposely seek their graduates. Although this experience can be difficult to manage, the potential positive impact far outweighs the difficulty of the experience. It is important, however, to prepare for potential sensory overload.

The structure and flow of the career fair could be very overwhelming for someone with ASD. This large room will be filled with several conversations, a variety of displays at each table, free giveaways, students and representatives with perfume or cologne on, and many people could be gathered in the room at the same time. The impact of sensory overload is quite possible if not prepared for in advance. Take the following into account as you prepare for taking part in the career fair at your college:

- Study the career fair map to identify the companies of interest prior to the event.

- Research the companies involved.

- Have several clean copies of your current resume.

- Make a business card for yourself with your relevant information.

- Dress as you would for a job interview.

- Have a list of relevant questions prepared.

- Be prepared to shake hands with many people (have a hand sanitizer if needed).

- Most companies will have free giveaways, but **only take one**.

- Put a pleasant-smelling lotion under your nose to focus your sense of smell.

- Use ear plugs to drown out the chatter and extra noise.

- Work with the career center to identify less busy times to participate.

- Plan to spend a maximum of five minutes with each company representative, unless he or she engages you further.

- Collect business cards for follow-up.

- Be engaged while having conversations.

- Network with others while waiting for representatives.

- If the companies offer workshops, attend all that you can so you can be seen.

- Always say thank you.

- Have your personal sales pitch prepared and practiced.

For opportunities like a career fair, a personal sales pitch may be how you can sell yourself to a company quickly while others are trying to do the same. You will have the first 30 seconds with the representative to encourage him or her to be interested in you. During this time, you want them to have an understanding of your strengths, skill set, and goodness of fit with their company. This personal sales pitch should be scripted and practiced far in advance of the career fair. It should be something you are very comfortable and confident in reciting in the spur of the moment, and it could be the thing that gets you an initial interview. This introduction to yourself, followed by a strong resume, could be the key to career fair success.

The following elements should be included in your personal sales pitch:

- clear full name

- intended graduation date

- intended degree

- experience/internships

- specialized skill set

- mention of information gathered through research

- how your interests/skills meet the company's needs

- established "goodness of fit."

SAMPLE PERSONAL SALES PITCH SCRIPT

"Hello, my name is John Smith. I plan to graduate in May of 2016 with a Bachelor's degree in Computer Science. I was lucky enough to do a full internship with Unum Insurance Company as part of their software engineering department. While at this internship, I was able to use my specific skills of observation for details and creative problem-solving to automate processes that were previously manual. I believe that many companies value delivering the end product in the most effective and efficient manner to benefit them, and I believe my specific set of skills can help you do just that. I hope that you can see from my resume, that we may be a good professional fit for each other. It is very good to meet you and I look forward to discussing my potential with your company."

Your scripted personal sales pitch:

_____

_____

_____

_____

_____

_____

_____

In preparation for a career fair, practice this speech several times with a variety of people and in a variety of locations. Regardless of where you may be or with whom you may be conversing, it is important that you can deliver this speech with confidence and strength. Practice as many times as necessary to be able to deliver this pitch flawlessly to anyone with whom you speak.

Another potential tool for success would be for you to video yourself delivering your personal sales pitch. Take notes of your verbal fluidity and your body movements as you deliver the speech. Identify specific things you can improve on to make your speech come across with more confidence. This 30-second speech could be the determining factor that sets you aside from other job seekers.

LESSON 4: NETWORKING WITH PROFESSIONALS

Professional networking is a method of increasing the number of people in your potential career who know you and who have an understanding of your skill set and interests. The more people who know you and know your strengths, the better chance you will have at landing an interview. Increasing your sphere of opportunities beyond your direct daily contacts correlates with a greater number of referrals and potential career placements. Networking has typically been viewed as an informal and very social activity, which has been what has steered many individuals with ASD away from this experience. Some professional networking experiences continue in this way, although there are other opportunities for networking that are framed differently.

Many companies now use networking strategies as their primary marketing and recruiting method. Instead of investing money into recruitment and advertising, they pull from their own professional referral network. This network has possibly been developed through one-off meetings with people who have discovered something interesting about an individual, who then refer that individual to someone who has a similar interest or skill. As an individual with many significant strengths and specific skills, your information could sit with a number of professionals who could pull your name out as a referral for a job before anyone even advertises for an opening. If your information is passed on as a referral, the likelihood of you being granted an initial interview is heightened significantly.

As you begin your career search, it is worth noting that you could meet someone who could be a valuable member of your professional network anywhere. You could meet someone in a class who has an influential family member, you could impress a guest lecturer who may refer you on graduation, you could attend a career fair and meet someone in line who has a professional mentor who could help you make connections, or you could attend and/or present at professional conferences to share your work. It is possible that you could even meet someone at a restaurant or on an airplane who has similar interests to you and who could have a significant professional influence on your career trajectory.

Networking activities are not always designed. Instead, they are often a case of first impressions being strong. You can never change a first impression, however, so at this point in your college/career path you should be concerned with making a good first impression at all times. It is a good idea to make business cards with your contact information, and to have current, clean copies of your resume with you at all times. You should make it a habit to ask for other people's business cards when you interact with those who could help you professionally. By gathering business cards and writing notes on the back regarding business interests and affiliations, use these contacts to further your job search as well as helping others make professional contacts. Your referrals could also be valuable in helping others build professionals connections.

Using social media as a networking tool can be highly valuable. Sites such as LinkedIn can allow for you to highlight your professional strengths and skills while also allowing you to celebrate what sets you aside from others. Setting up a profile on

LinkedIn takes very little time and can accomplish what typically previously had to be done through the formal recruitment and interview process. By sharing your resume and getting endorsements from respected people, you can bypass many of the initial stages of the recruitment process. Your connections on LinkedIn can be viewed through the same lens as professional referrals you may meet with in person. These connections can be gained through joining groups of interest and reading the profiles of others within the group. Each contact has their own professional network of connections that may then reach out to you to connect. This structure of building a professional network through social media decreases the requirement to be consistently socially proficient during possibly important interactions, and allows a person with ASD to enjoy similar benefits from professional networking that may come much easier for neurotypical peers.

The first step in developing a profile for social media networking is similar to delivering a personal sales pitch. The summary at the start of your profile should be thick with content, outlining all those things that make you the person people want to connect with. It should include the things that define you personally and professionally, as well as the specific skills in which you have mastery. It is often difficult for a person with ASD to share their positive qualities, but this is a requirement in building a profile. Reflect on the things that people have identified as your strengths. In what areas have you experienced success? What topics do you particularly enjoy researching and working through? What tasks are you often recruited to complete? These are the questions you can answer through your narrative to begin building your social media profile.

Research the LinkedIn profiles of people within your chosen field, and document what they have outlined as their strengths. Begin work on developing your professional narrative, and plan to use this information to develop a variety of professional accounts on social media for the purpose of networking.

Profiles are divided into five main sections: summary, experience, skills, education, and recommendations. Each section is important and should be addressed equally. Use the following examples to develop your own profile to begin your professional networking on social media.

Summary

This section allows you to develop a narrative about who you are as a professional. It is similar to your professional sales pitch about yourself. The following is an example of a brief professional summary:

I am a goal-oriented person who strives for equality for all people. I love program development that encourage people with disabilities to fully participate in all that life has to offer. I am an advocate, leader, teacher, and squeaky wheel when I need to be.

  Someone once wrote that to be a good leader in higher ed, you have to be a dove, a dragon and a diplomat. I tend to live my professional life as a diplomat, always negotiating on behalf of people with disabilities. When people treat others with disabilities in a discriminatory fashion, I can quickly become a dragon. The thing that makes me a dove is what drives my passion every single day. Working with the amazingly talented and honest students in the MoSAIC Program. This is always a challenge, but incredibly rewarding as well.

Experience

This section of your profile is very similar to a resume. You can build in any professional experiences you may have, including volunteer work, internships, or paid employment.

University of Tennessee at Chattanooga
Access Coordinator, Disability Resource Center
University of Tennessee, Chattanooga
May 2014–Present (1 year), Chattanooga, TN

University of Tennessee, Chattanooga
Instructor, USTU 1999, MoSAIC Social Strategies
University of Tennessee, Chattanooga
September 2013–Present (1 year 8 months)

Skills

This section is a developed for you to highlight the skills you see as your strengths. The connections you make through this social media site will then have the opportunity to endorse your skill set. The following is a list of skills highlighted by a user of social media networking. The numbers to the left identify how many people have endorsed that skill.

Skills
4 Psychology
3 Higher education
2 Program development
2 Student affairs
1 Student development
1 Academic advising

Education

This section allows you to highlight your academic successes. This could include your degrees, academic honors, GPA, etc. The following example displays this vital information:

University of Tennessee, Chattanooga
EdD, Learning and Leadership, 2009–13
GPA 3.9

Prescott College
M.A., Special Education Administration, 2000–03
GPA 4.0

Western Michigan University
BS, Exceptional Education, 1992–98
Magna Cum Laude

Recommendations

This section allows people in your professional referral network to endorse you and share your strengths from their perspective. It can carry much importance, as this is another professional talking about your skills. You will need to ask someone to write this recommendation for you, but these tend to be very well received on many social media networking sites. The following is an example of a recommendation written for the purpose of social media networking:

"Michelle is an excellent colleague who has given much of her precious time to me to learn more about students, faculty, and staff with disabilities. Michelle collaborated on an International Service Course I teach by including four students identifying as on the autism spectrum. I highly recommend Michelle as a resource in higher education."

FIGURE 7.1 AN EXAMPLE OF A SOCIAL MEDIA PROFILE

Take some time to develop each section of your potential social media networking profile and comment on potential connections in groups.

Summary:

Experience:

Skills:

Education:

Recommendations:

Potential connections on social media:

_____

_____

_____

_____

_____

_____

Potential groups to join:

_____

_____

_____

_____

_____

_____

BACK TO BASICS

Consider these guiding questions as you prepare to evaluate yourself.

B 1 2 3	**Behavior**	Are you exploring career options? Are you exploring jobs you find interesting? Have you job shadowed anyone in a field related to your interests? Are you reaching out to your community when looking for opportunities?
A 1 2 3	**Academics**	Are you managing your time, balancing career exploration and coursework? Are you applying organizational strategies? Do you have realistic expectations for your future? Are you preparing for a career fair or other networking opportunities on campus? Are you attending career fairs?
S 1 2 3	**Self-care**	Are you keeping yourself motivated? Are you eating healthily? Are you planning for your self-care activities? Are you using your time management strategies? Are you maintaining a professional image?
I 1 2 3	**Interaction**	Are you checking in with your support team? Are you networking? Are you looking for opportunities in your community? Do others see you as motivated? Do you feel connected?
C 1 2 3	**Community**	Do you value others when in a team? Are you staying connected within your community? Are you asking questions to those already in the field? Are you utilizing your support team to help you get connected? Are you accepting critical feedback?
S 1 2 3	**Self-monitoring**	Is your energy equally distributed between career search and academics? Are you thinking of your passion and special interest as you work on your career exploration? Are you marketing yourself? Are you advocating for yourself? Are you being mindful about the topics you should discuss with caution?

⬇ **BACK TO BASICS: RATE YOURSELF**

B Behavior 1 2 3	Comments
A Academics 1 2 3	Comments
S Self-care 1 2 3	Comments
I Interaction 1 2 3	Comments
C Community 1 2 3	Comments
S Self- monitoring 1 2 3	Comments

GOALS

Personal:

Academic:

Social:

Chapter 8

INTERNSHIPS AND STRATEGICALLY PLANNING FOR THE FUTURE

INTRODUCTION

Internships, while certainly not always required, can be integral to the career development for young adults with ASD. Because intern–supervisor relationships are mutually beneficial to both parties, the structure of the internship is set up so that students are supported and have the potential to truly impact the operations of the internship company in a positive way. Some are paid and some are not, some may be available or even required through courses at colleges, and others will be identified and pursued through individual student effort. As students with ASD consider their future employment interests, internships are one way to learn about the field and work environment while receiving support and feedback along the way.

Knowing the general process for obtaining and maintaining an internship can be essential for students with ASD. On the one hand, it prepares students for the multiple elements of the internship application and interview process. On the other, students can acknowledge how ASD might impact them in the potential internship arenas. Guiding students through the process, with individual action steps, will allow them to focus on their strengths and how best to demonstrate them rather than sightlessly encountering the internship process.

As students with ASD consider internship possibilities, they can utilize their campus resources to set up support. Students can seek out support from others during all stages of the internship process, from researching potential placements to arranging for the presentation of a culminating internship project. Emphasizing resourcefulness on their own behalf, students are asked to frame their support system for internships throughout this chapter.

Just as the availability of support can be a reason for pursuing internships as a young adult with ASD, the opportunity for valuable feedback presents another fortunate aspect of internship structures. As students are exploring their career options, feedback can be a tool providing direction. ASD may impact some of the soft skills needed for the workplace environment and social interactions, so it is especially important for young adults on the spectrum to be open to feedback and to actively seek it out. Internships allow for support, feedback, and career readiness in a partnership designed to facilitate the development of the intern.

LESSON 1: PROCESS AWARENESS

When you were first considering college, you likely did quite a bit of preparation work to learn how the transition would go before you arrived on campus. In much the same way, you will need to prepare for internships and understand the process you would go through to obtain one. Since you may have difficulty with transitions as a young adult on the spectrum, you can avoid being surprised by internship elements and burdened with confusion during the process by doing some background work to prepare yourself for what is to come. Diving blindly into internship work without properly preparing can lead to making unfortunate impressions on potential employers. In addition, if you are unprepared, the likelihood of obtaining a position is minimal, and you will have wasted an opportunity to build your resume and gain field experience. You have worked through an understanding of what internships are and how they are involved in the career continuum, but this lesson explores the steps of the internship process further.

One aspect of the internship process to be mindful of, as with most career processes, is seeking a good fit for you so you can demonstrate your talents and skills. This awareness is key to the process of planning for an internship. While experience is certainly always worthwhile, not all options will be right for you. Ideally, you could apply and have offers for internships from which you can choose instead of taking your first offer. Even if you prioritize internship effort, there is a chance that your placement will not work out. As a student with ASD, be especially cognizant of how well your internship placement correlates with your goals and the support you may receive.

There are many individual steps that can be taken to pursue an internship, and these steps may be taken in varying orders or skipped over entirely by some students. Generally, though, the process is very similar to the general career or job search process outlined in this book. Many of the components of both processes are the same and they may occur in a similar order, but because internships differ from other positions, the process looks slightly more defined.

There are seven steps in the internship progression that highlight some of its fundamental components. Read through the descriptions of each basic step, and then complete the extra bullets.

1. Research: Before you can move on to exploring any other element in the internship process, find out what opportunities are available. As a college student, you have access to resources on campus to help you identify possible internship placements. Creating a plan for how to compile research information about different companies will allow you to consistently organize research for new positions in your community. Consider whether each opportunity is realistic for you based on your analysis of factors like internship requirements, interest–skill match, academic credit or stipend availability, and the duration of the internship. Only by taking the time to research your opportunities will you find an internship that fits your needs and that of the placement company.

2. Prepare: As you narrow down your potential internship interests, the next step is to begin preparing for the application process. Before applying to any internship, adjust your resume to highlight the appropriate information for each internship possibility. Clarify contact information and important deadlines for application materials. Have everything you will need for the application ready before moving on to the next step. Become familiar with your work and education history, as the application will ask you to describe it. Your goal while you prepare at this stage is to gather information about the application process and the company in which you are interested. Knowing as much as you can will help ensure that you successfully navigate the next few steps.

3. Apply: Applying for an internship is obviously one of the most important elements of the internship progression. Your college may have been a resource for you during the search process, and they can also aid in the application process. Be sure to clarify any aspect of the application for any internship with others if you have questions. The application process will likely include some type of a fill-in-the-blank form, which may be online, asking you to identify and describe your basic qualifications and other information. It will also include a request for your resume and references. Understand that you might not be notified of your application status, so you may wish to follow up with the application recipient after this step to ensure all materials have arrived and, if a decision is pending, find out when you might be notified of the next step in the process so you can prepare accordingly.

4. Interview: In Chapter 6 you explored interviews in depth, and you can use what you learned then in this step of the internship process. An internship supervisor conducts interviews with potential candidates for the same reasons an employer would interview a potential job candidate. If you have been asked to interview for an internship after submitting your application, this means that you are a candidate for the internship, and the supervisor's decision depends on more information from you in the form of an interview. He or she, or the group, in your interview will be observing your behavior and hearing your responses in order to discern if you are a good fit for the internship. Essentially, the biggest takeaway from this step is that you should treat the internship interview as if it were for your dream job.

5. Follow Up: After you have interviewed for an internship, it is a good idea to follow up with those who interviewed you. Taking the time to say "thank you" for the opportunity to interview is one of the more common interview etiquette responsibilities. Another reason you may wish to follow up is to clarify your response to a certain question that was asked in the interview. This may be particularly important if you have arranged to do so to accommodate for processing difficulties (which can be an impact of ASD), which interfere with

your responses. This follow-up step is also a chance for you to inquire about the next stage in the process, in particular when and how you will be notified.

6. Commit: If you are offered an internship, the next step is a decision you have to make. Knowing the commitment that any internship is, you will need to clarify and obtain details about the internship you have been offered. In the event that you are offered more than one internship, this step becomes more complicated, because you will need to choose which internship is the best fit for you. Before committing and accepting an internship offer, consider all the details that you need to be aware of as you enter the experience. There will be a limit to how much time you may take to provide your supervisor with your commitment, so even as you apply, consider whether this is an internship you would be glad to have.

7. Evaluate: The last step, evaluating your performance at the internship, is more continuous. Since at this stage you are an intern, your focus should be on your performance in the workplace. In order to regularly gather information about how you are doing and what support you may need, evaluating yourself as an intern is essential and promotes accountability. Practicing self-monitoring in a career setting allows you to recognize patterns in your behavior or work that may cause concern, so you can adjust these as you go along. Seeking feedback from your supervisor is another way to evaluate your progress from a different perspective. Internships are learning opportunities for interns, so evaluations will also give you feedback about the work tasks or social skills on which you can improve. Evaluating your work and requesting feedback from supervisors is a career skill you will apply in an internship and continue to practice throughout your career.

For the activities for this lesson you will identify action steps for the internship progression. The seven steps are outlined on the following page, and one action step for each is provided, so your task is to refer to this lesson and other research to define the other action steps that you need to take to be successful at each step.

THE SEVEN STEPS TO INTERNSHIP SUCCESS

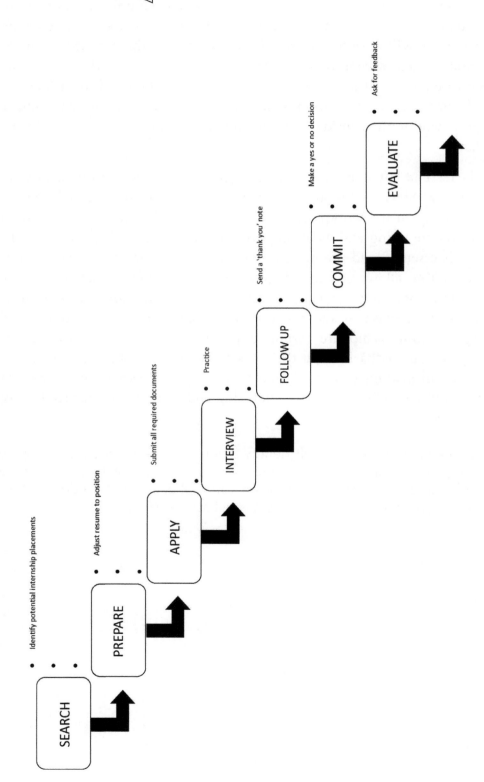

INTERNSHIP SUCCESS

SEARCH

Identify potential internship placements

PREPARE

Adjust resume to position

APPLY

Submit all required documents

INTERVIEW

Practice

FOLLOW UP

Send a 'thank you' note

COMMIT

Make a yes or no decision

EVALUATE

Ask for feedback

LESSON 2: SETTING UP SUPPORT

As a college student, an internship is a way to gain experience in a field that interests you while you are still taking classes and managing your campus social life. Knowing that you have many responsibilities during the process of acquiring and then maintaining a role as an intern, you can engage with others to receive support throughout the process, making it all feel a little less overwhelming. Identifying and connecting with supportive people on your campus and at your internship, determining any need for accommodations while you are an intern, and establishing communication methods for support are all ways you can improve your chances of being successful at your internship.

Depending on how ASD impacts you, your support group may be composed of various people, and these supportive relationships may each be rooted to individual goals. For example, perhaps another intern whose desk is nearby understands ASD and supports you by being a point person you can depend on to interpret social cues in the workplace. Another example that portrays the way your support group changes may be that your academic advisor at college supports you by having routine meetings with you to relate internship material to your college courses. Each of these two examples of supportive people would help you in different ways regarding your internship, and it is up to you to decide who your support is and how it will exist. Your support will come from many angles in your life while you are an intern, so you will need to identify and establish intentional connections with possible supportive resources.

One support you may seek out is work-related accommodations through the supervisor for whom you are working at your internship. Accommodations at work are like those you might have had for the impact of ASD in your college classes. The provision of accommodations is determined by various factors, but it is your responsibility to initiate this process. As an adult, you will be expected to advocate for yourself and your needs as an individual with ASD. Accommodations can support you in several ways, but what accommodations are reasonable is individually established through your internship placement, and the specific ways ASD or other disabilities you may have impact you. Learning more about the work environment will help you to discern whether accommodations will be something that you need to seek out as an intern. Likewise, analyzing the environment and your tasks, and considering the accommodation process as an intern, will help prepare you for the same during other experiences in your career development.

People and accommodations can certainly be instrumental to a valuable support system, but as a young adult in an internship position, you will need to learn how to support yourself in the role too. As an intern, you will need to particularly work to foster your ability to be resourceful. You are there to help, and it is important that you recognize that the extent to which you are able to help will be limited if you are always seeking to be helped yourself. While you can learn much during an internship from those with whom you work, depending too much on your support can lead to negative outcomes, and even possibly losing your internship position. A certain confidence comes from independently performing tasks and receiving a "job well done!" remark from those who are evaluating you. You will increasingly find that fostering resourcefulness in your daily interactions at your internship will prepare you for any number of potential tasks or questions.

Combining your resources with action is a goal you will need to have as you set up support for an internship. You know yourself better than anyone, so you can brainstorm about what you expect of yourself as an intern. Considering several factors that will be evaluated at an internship before you begin working in order to identify potential strengths or barriers to your success within the context of an internship can help you prepare for requesting reasonable support. After you have considered how you will fare in an internship in each of four categories (social interaction, communication, appearance, and job performance), compare your notes with someone who can provide feedback about you in these categories from their perspective, to create a more complete understanding of your internship support needs. From this exercise, you can create scripts or narratives that you can use to guide your conversations with supervisors regarding how they can support you during your internship.

In each category, consider the following:

1. Social interaction: Are there aspects of social interactions that pose a difficulty for you? What are they? What are your strengths in social interactions with others, particularly in the work setting? Have you ever received support in the area of social interaction in the workplace before? If so, describe the support.

2. Communication: How do you prefer to communicate with professionals? What communication method is best received when you are seeking feedback? Are there any communication challenges that you foresee impacting your performance at your internship?

3. Appearance: How do you expect your appearance to change when you are at your internship from how you appear as a student? Are you aware of your personal hygiene and its impact on appearance? Do you have support in your personal life to help you maintain appropriate internship appearance?

4. Job performance: At which tasks do you expect to perform well? How do you describe your work ethic? In terms of competency, what about your potential performance as an intern concerns you?

Considering these four elements, complete the Internship Brainstorming Plan that follows. First, fill in your internship expectations for yourself in the four categories. Then ask a mentor, faculty member, or someone else who knows you well in a professional setting to add notes about you in the four categories. Using the two perspectives, you can build a narrative from which you can seek additional support from your supervisor. To do so, for each category, you will need to develop a script as if you were to provide this information to your supervisor. Whether or not you use the script in your internship to set up support is up to you, but it can be a useful tool for you to recognize how owning and explaining your expectations and characteristics can lead to meaningful and supportive relationships with those people surrounding you at your internship.

INTERNSHIP BRAINSTORMING PLAN

Social interaction:

_____

_____

_____

_____

_____

_____

_____

_____

_____

Narrative:

_____

_____

_____

_____

_____

_____

_____

_____

_____

_____

Communication:

_____

_____

_____

_____

_____

_____

_____

_____

_____

_____

_____

Narrative:

_____

_____

_____

_____

_____

_____

_____

_____

_____

_____

_____

_____

Appearance:

_____

_____

_____

_____

_____

_____

_____

_____

_____

_____

Narrative:

_____

_____

_____

_____

_____

_____

_____

_____

_____

_____

Job performance:

_____

_____

_____

_____

_____

_____

_____

_____

_____

_____

Narrative:

_____

_____

_____

_____

_____

_____

_____

_____

_____

_____

_____

LESSON 3: RECEIVING FEEDBACK

As an intern, you will be expected to learn quickly and to understand the working world specific to the company. In order to learn and adapt to your internship responsibilities, you can receive feedback that will guide you as you continually work to improve. As a student with ASD, you will want to be especially aware of the feedback you receive as it can help you understand your progress with some of the workplace elements that may cause anxiety or stress for you. Feedback at your internship will indicate your strengths and the aspects of the role that you could improve on. As you transition to your role as an intern, you will need to seek feedback from many angles. Look to those around you for nonverbal feedback about your progress, directly ask for situational feedback, and set up ways to regularly receive feedback from your supervisors.

When it comes to receiving feedback from those around without actually asking for it, recall what you know about social cues. If you choose not to disclose to your co-workers that you have ASD, being mindful of how those around you are treating you in response to your work or behavior is one way you can receive feedback. For example, assume that when you first start your internship your supervisors patiently answer frequent questions about tasks. After a few weeks, though, your supervisor starts avoiding you or closing their office to you, giving shorter and curter responses to your questions, telling you to write the answer down so you don't have to ask again. In this example you could use the feedback from your supervisor to evaluate your behavior, and come to the conclusion that your learning period is ending and you are now expected to ask fewer questions. Feedback that is less direct can sometimes be difficult to ascertain, so take note of the ways responses to your work and behavior change. Ask for clarification about the feedback you interpret if you need to, but be sure to write down the responses so you will not have to clarify them again.

Another way to receive feedback is to simply ask for it. As an intern who is learning in the field, you may require situational feedback to mediate potential issues. Additionally, you may evaluate your work by asking for feedback about a project that you completed, so you can know what to improve on for future projects.

Asking for feedback as an intern should only occur when you absolutely need it, because your supervisor and co-workers are going to be busy with their own work. It can be easy when you first start a new internship position to ask for feedback about every element of your work, but be selective about the feedback you request. If possible, exhaust all other resources before going directly to a supervisor to request situational feedback. As you develop in the field, your need for feedback may decrease, but realize that all employees seek feedback about their progress. You are not expected to know all of the answers all of the time as an intern. In fact, you are there to learn and to grow with the experience, but remember that your supervisor has to first perform his or her job in order to be able to address your concerns and offer feedback and suggestions.

Setting up regular support through consistent, scheduled feedback sessions with your supervisor is an arrangement that could make receiving feedback more structured for both parties involved. Your supervisor may not have much experience working with individuals on the spectrum, so this type of supportive routine could help your supervisor respond to your needs, and also understand how an intern with ASD is a terrific asset to the team. Working in a structured setting with the singular objective of receiving feedback about your progress will make the process easier for you to really gather knowledge and to move on from the meeting having learned how to improve your skills in the work setting. Regular feedback meetings are common between interns and supervisors as they provide a space to discuss progress, propose changes, establish helpful strategies, clarify tasks, and address issues within the organized context of a scheduled meeting.

Support can begin once you are aware of your needs and able to communicate them in a way that addresses concerns specifically related to your work as an intern and the setting in which you do this work. Once you have self-evaluated your progress, you may compare your own evaluation to that of your supervisor. Providing some of the areas where young adults with ASD need feedback—like social interaction, communication, appearance, and job performance—can direct the feedback you receive. An evaluation form can be provided to your supervisor that mimics the self-evaluation that you will have completed. Asking your supervisor to fill out the form to give you feedback in areas that might cause concern for you can simplify the process for them. Direct the feedback you receive by designing questions that seek to evaluate the aspects of internships that you are actively working to improve.

In the following activity, Internship Evaluation, you will practice self-evaluation and requesting feedback using a pre-designed form. This form allows for feedback about your social interactions, communication, appearance, and job performance. A rating scale from "unacceptable" to "mastered" adds perspective to the responses so you are able to see how to improve. Make a copy of the form, and complete the internship evaluation for yourself and also have your supervisor complete it. Remember that this can guide the structured meetings you have to receive supportive feedback.

INTERNSHIP EVALUATION

Intern: _____   Date: _____

Supervisor: _____

	Unacceptable → Average → Mastered				
Social interaction					
Handles stress well	1	2	3	4	5
Makes eye contact	1	2	3	4	5
Refrains from social infractions (e.g. excessive talking)	1	2	3	4	5
Admits mistakes	1	2	3	4	5
Accepts praise	1	2	3	4	5
Cooperative and courteous	1	2	3	4	5
Communication					
Listens and pays attention	1	2	3	4	5
Expresses personal needs	1	2	3	4	5
Respects the rights and privacy of others	1	2	3	4	5
Asks for help when needed	1	2	3	4	5
Appearance					
Maintains clean appearance	1	2	3	4	5
Dresses appropriately for the job	1	2	3	4	5
Has good general hygiene	1	2	3	4	5
Job performance					
Follows directions	1	2	3	4	5
Accepts constructive criticism/feedback	1	2	3	4	5
Follows rules and regulations	1	2	3	4	5
Asks for help when needed	1	2	3	4	5
Maintains good attendance	1	2	3	4	5

	Unacceptable → Average → Mastered				
Arrives on time for work/leaves on time	1	2	3	4	5
Attentive to the job at hand	1	2	3	4	5
Completes task accurately	1	2	3	4	5
Works well with co-workers	1	2	3	4	5
Initiates new tasks	1	2	3	4	5

Comments

LESSON 4: THE POSSIBILITIES

For a young adult, completing an internship is a rewarding experience in terms of career preparation. Even if your experience as an intern dismantles your notion of the type of job you might pursue later on, or does not lead directly to a full-time employment opportunity, you will have learned about the basic and fundamental work elements of a certain field. As a student with ASD, internships allow you to investigate potential work environments, explore the unspoken social rules that guide interactions, and attain significant amounts of knowledge in a field. Beyond that, though, internships have the potential to open many doors to you while you are still a student.

Imagine interning for a business for six months, fetching coffee for higher-ranked co-workers in between taking notes for executive meetings and responding to customer service emails. At the end of six months, your internship supervisor invites you in for an end-of-internship evaluation, and you learn that you have impressed the company and they wish to hire you as a paid employee. If you accept, you would be working part-time hours with the opportunity for advancement. This narrative evokes the kind of possibilities that students with ASD have to consider when approaching their career. Internships amplify possible career outcomes for students in college.

A new job after an internship is a goal that many young adults consider as an experience worthy of the effort. This possibility can shift into reality for interns who fit the mold of the company's ideal candidate for a position. Similar to other promotions, being offered a paid employment position on completing an internship is attributed to hard work and professional fit. Investing your time and effort in an internship demonstrates to your supervisor that you value the opportunity, and if you are a good fit and an entry-level position is available, your supervisor could very well advance you along in your career.

Whether or not a new position is awarded on completion of an internship, the people with whom you have interacted in that role are now part of your professional network. Networking as an intern delivers the possibility for an array of potential career development experiences. In many cases as an intern, you may work in conjunction with other interns who share similar interests and are positioned similarly in terms of career growth. At other times you will work alongside a more senior representative of the company, and assist this person directly. In both cases, the social interactions you have with them matter, as you should be aware that their impression of you could impact the potential networking relationships you may have with them. As your professional communication techniques improve from practice at your internship, networking will be easier to manage. Being in the new work setting and interacting with those around you at your internship may initially create some stress, but as you spend time adjusting, your professional approach to the workplace will be more and more appropriate. Increasing your own professionalism can improve how well you are able to network and expand the possibilities of your internship.

Finally, internships, despite all the benefits they posit for you as a young adult with ASD, are not guaranteed fits. One internship outcome possibility is that you realize that the role, or the field entirely, is not for you. In the event that you are dissatisfied with an internship, you may reconsider other options for work in the same field, but at a different company doing different work. But before dismissing your academic major or changing your career goals from the ground up because of one bad experience at an internship in the field, go back to your seven-step internship progression guide and begin with research (see page 151). Figure out what other opportunities there are for you in the field, and try to arrange internships in another role. While internships do not always lead to a new job, or an automatic vast network of professionals, young adults with ASD can move on from the experience having learned even if the knowledge relates more to satisfaction with your career direction than information about the field.

For the activity in this lesson (Internship Outcome Possibilities), you will simply need to consider potential outcomes for an internship. There are three possibilities outlined on the left, so you should first brainstorm and write in three other possible outcomes on the right. Then, take it a bit further to explore the next possibility from each outcome.

INTERNSHIP OUTCOME POSSIBILITIES

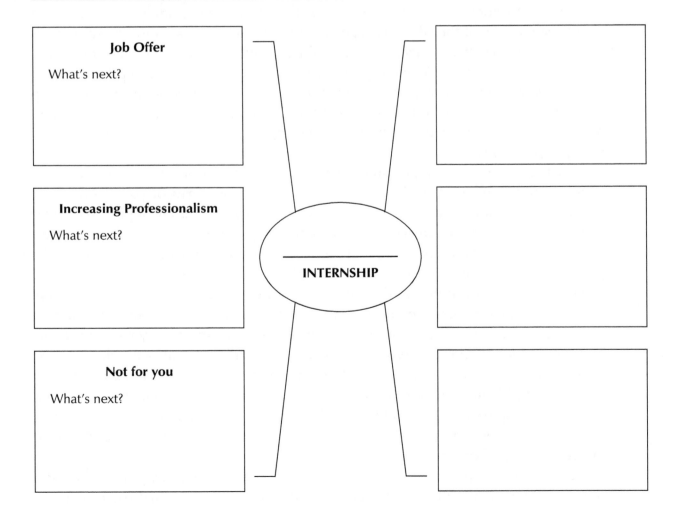

The possible outcomes for students with ASD who pursue and complete internships depend on many factors, but all encompass some degree of increased career readiness and self-awareness. Any effort you put into career preparation, like going through the process of identifying and applying for internships, contributes to your overall development in ways beyond merely being career-focused. The social skills demanded by career preparation strategies can be applied to many interactions in your adult life. A structured and interesting environment like an internship is one opportunity in which you can practice these skills and receive feedback, preparing your further for a successful career.

BACK TO BASICS

Consider these guiding questions as you prepare to evaluate yourself.

B	**Behavior** 1 2 3	Are you completing internship/internship preparation tasks? Do you engage consistently with others? Do you ask for help when you need it? Are you increasing your resourcefulness?
A	**Academics** 1 2 3	Are you aware of academic requirements for internships? Do you meet with your advisor regularly? Are you keeping with up your assignments? Are you organized and able to track your work and grades? Are you utilizing academic strengths at your internship?
S	**Self-care** 1 2 3	Are you getting enough sleep? How are you planning for self-care activities? Are you spending time doing things you enjoy? Do you have time to complete personal errands? Are you aware of the accommodations you need?
I	**Interaction** 1 2 3	Are you engaging socially with internship co-workers? Are you looking for opportunities in your community? Do you notice how others respond to you? Are your interactions positive?
C	**Community** 1 2 3	Are you engaged with your network? Who can support you during this process? Do you support your community? Are you aware of campus resources for internships? How can you engage with your local community?
S	**Self-monitoring** 1 2 3	Are you managing your time? Are you accepting critical feedback? Do you manage your stress and frustration well? Are you advocating for yourself? Are you organized and on time for appointments?

BACK TO BASICS: RATE YOURSELF

B	**Behavior** 1 2 3	**Comments**
A	**Academics** 1 2 3	**Comments**
S	**Self-care** 1 2 3	**Comments**
I	**Interaction** 1 2 3	**Comments**
C	**Community** 1 2 3	**Comments**
S	**Self-monitoring** 1 2 3	**Comments**

GOALS

Personal:

Academic:

Social:

Chapter 9

ALTERNATE PATHS

INTRODUCTION

Our effort to help prepare young adults with ASD for life after college would be amiss if we did not discuss alternate paths. Not every college student graduates and goes directly into a career. Graduate school, studying abroad, taking time off, working a series of jobs, or learning new life skills necessary for independent living without the structure of college are all possibilities. While there are valuable lessons to be learned in the workplace, young adults with ASD can also benefit from an array of other post-college experiences. The possibilities truly are endless, but this chapter discusses graduate school, study abroad, the purpose of a job vs. a career, and potential pitfalls. Whether or not these are the experiences young adults choose, exploring their potential can lead to a more in-depth knowledge of their career aspirations and the skills that need to be developed.

Because all students bring unique perspectives to a discussion of alternate paths, this chapter provides opportunities to explore new experiences even if their path is more career-focused directly out of college. Students should read through this chapter and complete the activities in each lesson as if they were planning to go to graduate school, or as if they were planning to study or travel abroad. While students may not actually fulfill these elements of an alternate path, they can learn from the process of planning for them. After all, students could find that after a year or two in their career field after college that they would like to advance in the field by going to graduate school, or that they would like to travel to another region between employment positions. As students prepare to move forward through this chapter, they should consider how these lessons can be applied to their own lives. For example, planning for study abroad could help students consider the factors they would also need to know for planning a family vacation or helping themselves or co-workers make attending work-related conferences a reality.

For young adults with ASD, knowing what to expect with the coming events and transitions can ease stress when handling these new situations. Although there are no specific guidelines for acknowledging the diversions or interruptions that may interfere with the original plan for a career, students can take some steps to prepare for unexpected transitions. For some, potential pitfalls may occur in their career progression, which leaves them with the task of re-orienting their position in the career development process. Other young adults may find that they have addressed every piece of standard employment preparation they could muster, only to find that their plan has gone awry for uncontrollable reasons. For young adults with ASD, being willing to transfer strengths to new experiences despite any dismantling of the plan along the way will allow for better navigating the career exploration process.

LESSON 1: GRADUATE SCHOOL

Many students enter college with specific ideas of what their future career will be. Others begin their experience with little notion of their goals beyond achieving a college degree. One of the steps that students in both categories often consider is attending graduate school. For some, this is merely a step on a pre-designed path toward a certain identified career goal. Others see graduate school as a way to advance their knowledge while considering career options. As a student with ASD, you can benefit from already having experienced a transition in the college setting before graduate school, but you will also need to be prepared for the differences between obtaining an undergraduate degree and a graduate degree. Deciding to pursue a graduate degree underscores the fact that you are committing to more years and hours of serious academic work, and this should not be taken lightly. However, graduate school and advanced degrees can provide a platform for you as an individual with ASD to foster your own development in a particular field, and to develop professional skills that transfer to the workplace.

As a graduate student, you are responsible for adjusting to increased academic demands, presenting yourself as a professional representative of the program, and meeting consistently with the faculty to structure your individual experience. Considering your current experience in college academic courses should give you an idea of how you might fare in classes in graduate school that typically demand more work in less time. Not only will your grades need to be maintained at a higher level than was necessary for your undergraduate academic standing, but you will also be held to a different standard professionally.

Admission to graduate programs is contingent on your ability to manage the weight of responsibility that you commit to as a graduate student. Everyone around you will be paying for advanced instruction in a field that is specifically interesting to them, so they will also expect you, too, as a classmate, to be prepared and willing to participate in academic interactions. In particular, your professors at graduate level will expect you to be professional in your interactions, and academically conscientious.

Graduate school can be an incredibly beneficial undertaking, especially for students with ASD who desire more knowledge within the realm of their special interest areas, but committing to graduate-level work requires a plan.

If you are considering graduate school, take the time to research potential programs that interest you. Understand and practice explaining why you wish to study in a particular program so that you can work with the administrators and faculty who will be answering your questions. Talk to your current mentors, advisors, and instructors about their recommendations for graduate programs in your field. This is one example where your professional network can make a difference, so refer back to the contacts in your field if you need a place to begin your research. You can also work with these people to find out more about the demands of graduate school, and whether it is the right decision for you at this time, and you may even receive some tips for necessary graduate preparation examinations if they apply.

In addition to working with your professional network, you can learn quite a bit from doing some searching online to guide your basic research. First, think about how you would adjust your personal life to either continuing education with graduate school or returning to graduate school after an education hiatus. Here are some questions to guide your reflection:

- Will you need to maintain a part-time or full-time job to support yourself while you are in graduate school?

- If you do not have a job while you are studying, how will you support yourself as an independent adult?

- Are you willing to move to a different region to pursue study in your field?

- How will your routine change if your program requires an internship or field placement component?

- Does your decision to pursue graduate school directly affect the people you care about or your relationships?

Beyond those in your personal life, there are many factors that you need to consider as you research graduate school. Cost, program–career relation, admission requirements, course availability, and platform of delivery are just some of the elements in your graduate school research that you will need to keep track of in order to make a decision that makes the best impact on your future.

Complete the following table for a couple of potential graduate programs in your field (examples are provided). Compare your two options and keep track of your research.

RESEARCHING GRADUATE SCHOOL

	Example: State University	Option 1:	Option 2:
Program of Interest	Master's degree in Biology		
Cost	$10,500/year tuition (scholarships available)		
Admission Requirements	GPA: 3.5 80% score on entrance exam		
Deadlines	For Fall, due by April 6		
Course Availability	Online Evening hours Lab work required		
Professional Network	Email Dr. Land for biology club contact at S. U.		
Contact Information for Graduate Admissions	admissions@stuniv.edu		

LESSON 2: STUDY ABROAD

A unique opportunity that many college students take advantage of is studying in different parts of the world. Some examples of alternate paths for some students with ASD might be traveling for a semester in order to receive additional college credits, traveling for a week to celebrate undergraduate graduation, or traveling for a year while doing advanced studies in a field outside a university's physical region. If you are a young adult with ASD enrolling in a college course, resources are generally available on campus designed to help you individually navigate the study-abroad process. Developing your knowledge of the world while you study a subject that interests you in a new environment can be stimulating and can lead to newfound skills and increased independence.

There are many options as a young adult in college to travel, even if you are on a limited budget. If you are interested in traveling and studying, take some time to explore your options and set out to make your goals happen in a way that will prepare you for future opportunities.

One of the reasons why being a college student is beneficial when you consider traveling opportunities is because you have built-in support to help you structure your interest in pursuing them. On many campuses there are staff members who can help you with the many questions and concerns you might have about studying abroad. They may be able to help you identify potential programs for which you may qualify, outline the typical experience for a student studying abroad, and guide you through the application process. Other resources include your campus disability service office, which may have knowledge about study abroad opportunities that fit any needs you may have as someone with ASD, and your academic advisor, who could potentially point you toward options for studying abroad in your particular field. Similarly, another aspect of studying abroad in college is that you can tailor your travel to career goals, like internships.

Researching will help guide your decision about whether or not studying abroad is something you can realistically pursue. Remember to consider the implications all students face when studying abroad, like time away from family and friends, and potential delays in expected college graduation due to decreased course load while abroad, if applicable.

There are several factors you will need to start your basic research to decide if studying abroad is an option for you as an alternate path for you during career development. Here is a breakdown of five essential factors and corresponding questions you should consider:

1. College abroad: If you plan to study in your field, what are the colleges and universities that meet your needs in a location you find interesting? Explore possible routes for enrolling to take courses abroad, and be sure to research those universities that support the field you plan to enter.

2. Duration of study: How long are you willing to spend studying abroad? Think about how your financial resources impact this answer, and what the implications are regarding your graduation schedule, if this applies. If you have already graduated and plan to study abroad for an extended period of time, how can you also gain work experience?

3. Program cost: What are the tuition costs and additional fees for studying abroad in various programs and for varying durations? Remember that housing and other basic needs like food are generally not included in costs listed publicly, unless noted.

4. Application deadline: If you are planning to study abroad, what are the dates that you need to remember so you meet all necessary application deadlines? Consider whether all components are required at once or at different times. If you need to compile documents like recommendation letters from faculty members, note the dates by which you would need to receive those in order to pass them on in your application on time.

5. Relation to career field: Your study abroad opportunities might not always align with your career goals, but when they do, you can take advantage of unique experiences in your field that may apply to your future career. If possible, choose to study abroad in a way that emphasizes a particular skill or career interest you have so you can gain valuable travel experience while increasing your marketability.

On the next page, use the space provided to jot down notes about each of these factors for three potential study abroad destinations.

STUDY ABROAD DESTINATIONS

Draw a star where you would consider studying abroad. Do some research for your top three places.

★

College or University Abroad: _____

Duration of Study: _____

Program Cost: _____

Application Deadline: _____

Relation to career field: _____

★

College or University Abroad: _____

Duration of Study: _____

Program Cost: _____

Application Deadline: _____

Relation to career field: _____

★

College or University Abroad: _____

Duration of Study: _____

Program Cost: _____

Application Deadline: _____

Relation to career field: _____

LESSON 3: JOB VS. CAREER

Alternate paths to moving from college straight to a career provide an insight into different aspects of being a young adult with ASD for many students. A path that can be especially useful when preparing for a career is one along which you acquire and maintain a job or a series of jobs before settling into a focused career. Although it can be confusing, jobs and careers are not the same. Essentially, a job is what you do to earn a living, whereas a career is more like a general theme over the course of time toward your goals. Your career is the occupation you will hold, and a job is the act you will perform. These two terms will be used often in your research and career exploration, so be familiar with what they each mean.

A discussion of alternate paths in this chapter includes this distinction, as it will help you approach your next career-related move with more intention. As you grow as an individual and learn more about your interests and career goals, your trajectory may change. You may experience jobs in many different areas that may not necessarily align with what you intended when you set out.

One element of what sets a job apart from a career is that jobs do not represent your overall life goals the way a career does. While someone may have a job that contributes to their career goals, individuals can be identified more by their occupation and career (like a carpenter) than they are for the job they may have at the moment (such as a manager at a hardware store). As a young adult with ASD, it is important that you recognize that your goals may change as who you are as a person does. Gaining valuable experiences while you are a college student allows you to see how much your values and goals may change. Setting and reaching new goals with each job opportunity you have and while you are a student will guide you as you adjust to and refine your career aspirations.

While many people maintain jobs in their chosen field, some have a job simply in order to maintain independent living by being financially stable. There are certainly benefits to applying for and pursuing jobs that match your career aspirations, but there is rarely any harm in having a job from which you can learn valuable skills and experience potential workplace environments. Potential employers want to see that you have experience with the material you would be responsible for, in addition to being concerned with your ability to simply be a consistent and dependable employee. They will expect you to have at least a basic understanding of the way the operations work in a job, but they will also expect that every candidate will need some training.

As a student with ASD, consider the jobs you have had and how they apply to your goals and how they can help you develop the necessary skills to become an overall solid candidate for future opportunities in your career. In particular, think about how ASD has impacted you, and reflect on the ways you can demonstrate your strengths that will apply to any job.

Careers require discipline and strategic planning. They are developed over time as you invest in experiences that align with your life goals. You may have many jobs in your career, and even sometimes more than one career, but careers are long-term commitments.

Opportunities to increase your marketability within a career can include more than just adequate work exposure, but also those you activity seek out like attending conferences in your field, publishing articles for relevant academic journals, or taking the initiative to improve a certain job-specific skill. As you commit to your career and place value in it, seek these opportunities out, which will open doors to even more opportunities.

In the activity for this lesson, compare your general knowledge about the difference between a career and a job, recognizing how elements of both can assist you in your preparation work. Where a job and career overlap, you can see that they share some qualities that you can look for in all employment opportunities.

We have provided a few qualities that they share generally, and a few examples of how jobs and careers can individually provide significant experience for you as a young adult with ASD.

After taking a look at the example below, fill in the second diagram with any differences you have noted in jobs and careers, and how this knowledge might impact your career progression. Be sure to note that each experience will be different, and although each category will share some elements, accounting for these differences can help make you aware of how they impact you.

DIFFERENCE BETWEEN CAREER AND JOB

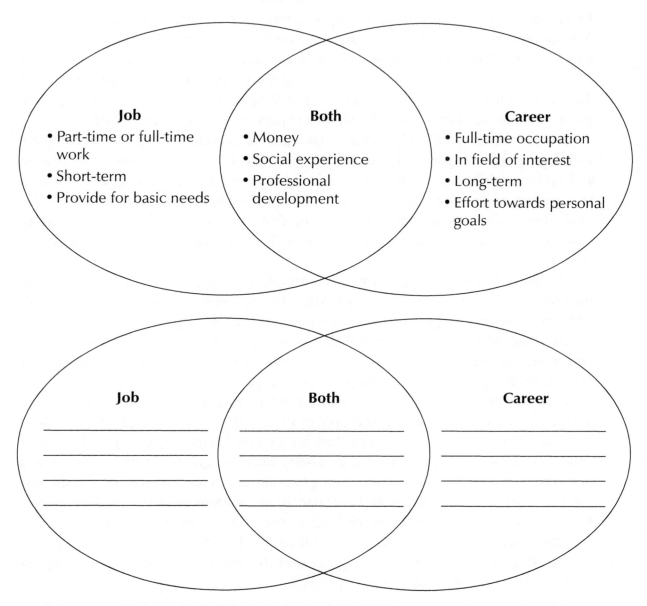

Job
- Part-time or full-time work
- Short-term
- Provide for basic needs

Both
- Money
- Social experience
- Professional development

Career
- Full-time occupation
- In field of interest
- Long-term
- Effort towards personal goals

Job

Both

Career

LESSON 4: POTENTIAL PITFALLS

As you begin exploring careers, the opportunities seem endless. As individuals with ASD often demonstrate, having a plan and routine makes transitions easier and can lessen stress. When pitfalls, or drawbacks, occur and disrupt a set plan, students with ASD need to recognize that adjusting to changes is simply an alternate path. Knowing that there are many ways to achieve an end goal despite the pitfalls, and becoming more aware of some common ones, will help you make the most of alternate paths.

Some common pitfalls might include taking an unexpectedly long time to complete a college degree, experiencing social isolation due to confusion about the process and options, mismanaging increased demands in academic and work areas of life as a young adult, and responding to academic mishaps that impact your plan or schedule for graduation. As a student with ASD, be aware that inevitable pitfalls that occur during your career preparation work will require flexibility and adapting to new needs as they are presented.

One pitfall that some students may encounter is taking longer than expected to complete the necessary degree requirements to graduate. Among many other reasons, students with ASD sometimes like longer to complete their degree because they take fewer courses each semester instead of a full course load that would allow for an earlier graduation date. Sometimes unexpected personal reasons contribute to the extension of college work. If you are already planning to take longer than your peers in college, be sure that you are working with an academic advisor to ensure you have access to the classes you need, and a schedule that allows for your best chance of success as you navigate your classes at your own pace. Being in college for longer than you expected could impact many elements of your experience at college, and could also delay career progression if your path involves obtaining positions for which there is an education or degree requirement. On the one hand, taking longer to graduate can have financial implications by increasing the semesters it takes to complete requirements, or limiting the financial assistance you receive each semester based on the hours in your course load. On the other hand, the additional time you spend in college before graduating increases the time you have to take advantage of the resources built into your campus experience.

While some students intentionally take longer to graduate and move on to a career or their next step, other students have to adjust their experience due to academic mishaps that create major career progression pitfalls. Essentially, failing even one class can lead to a spiraling academic mess. Maintaining a positive academic standing ensures that you are able to move on in your academic program in a timely manner by having fulfilled program requirements, by enrolling strategically in courses that may or may not have prerequisite course requirements. In some more extreme cases of academic difficulty while in college, students may even have to re-apply to continue taking courses.

These kind of academic dilemmas can lead to significant restructuring of a career plan. However, remember that academic pitfalls are common among all college students, and adjusting your effort and academic system to prevent similar mishaps in the future is one way to learn a valuable lesson of recovering from a pitfall that you can apply to future career experiences.

Another potential pitfall is social isolation that impacts other aspects of your life as a young adult. When your work effort and academic demands and social demands collide, this can lead to feeling overwhelmed, as though you can't keep up with all that is happening. As a student on the spectrum, one of the responses you may have to stress could be to avoid social events and situations in order to maintain a positive position in the work and academic areas of your life. Although social demands can increase the stress you may feel, it is better to seek support for navigating social nuances than to isolate yourself entirely. The people around you are valuable assets to you during your career efforts, and removing yourself from accessing their knowledge and support could be detrimental to your progress.

Having ASD, you may struggle with the skills that reinforce your ability to manage the multiple commitments in your life as a busy career-bound young adult. If you experience pitfalls related to managing this transition, like failing to keep track of deadlines for work and school and your social life, or receiving poor performance reviews or evaluations at your part-time job due to confusing work elements or tasks, first reflect on the structure you have in place for your daily life. Consider whether or not you need to adjust your schedule to include more time for one activity or less time for a more futile or less interesting activity in order to manage all your responsibilities. Understand that this is the adjustment period for the transition to adult responsibility beyond college, and that what effort you put into your personal development now is what you can carry with you throughout the series of career preparation strategies you go on to employ.

Alternate paths are common for students, with and without ASD, who, for one of many reasons, do not adhere to a standard career progression. The end goal and big picture, despite the time it takes to reach, or the events that transpire to interrupt progression toward it, will essentially be centered on your ability to independently provide for yourself and to live a satisfying life that allows you to do work that highlights your strengths in a field that interests you. Alternate paths just determine other ways of achieving your own end goal.

In the activity for this lesson, consider how different alternate paths can be analyzed as options. Explore some choices you may have during your time as a young adult in college, and identify the positive benefits (pros) and negative consequences (cons) to several factors that you must consider. Complete the activity by reflecting on the potential outcomes of decisions based on alternate paths and the pitfalls that may lead to them. Your own experience will represent your effort and any pitfalls that occur, but taking the time to practice responding and adapting to potential drawbacks to your plan can help you navigate the territory when you are inevitably faced with a similar decision.

As people make choices about which path to follow next, there is inevitably a potential for pitfalls. The best approach to making these difficult decisions is to complete a comprehensive "pros" and "cons" list. For each decision pair, identify some potential positive effects (pros) as well as the potential pitfalls (cons) of each decision.

ALTERNATIVE PATH COMPARISONS

Pros	Graduate on time	Cons
Example: Graduating on time allows entry into work world earlier	Graduate within five years according to graduation plan	Could miss out on potential extracurricular experiences
• • • • •		• • • • •

VS.

Pros	Study abroad	Cons
Example: Exposure to other cultures creates a larger sense of space within the world	Study abroad can put a student behind schedule academically, but provides a wealth of valuable experiences	Study abroad experiences are difficult to plan for and manage
• • • • •		• • • • •

vs.

Pros	Enter grad school	Cons
Example: More opportunities will be available with an advanced degree in the chosen field	Making the decision to enter graduate school means further education and obtaining an advanced degree	Graduate school often mean at least another two years of higher education tuition
•		•
•		•
•		•
•		•
•		•

Pros	Enter job search	Cons
Example: Beginning the job will potentially end in gainful employment	Entering the job search means searching for jobs before graduating with an undergraduate degree	Entering the job search with an undergraduate degree does not make a person marketable
•		•
•		•
•		•
•		•
•		•

Pros	Career focus	Cons
Example: Keeping a focus on the future will allow for "goodness of fit"	Focusing on developing a career takes longer, but has future implications	The process is longer and more time-intensive
•	•	•
•	•	•
•	•	•
•	•	•
•	•	•

vs.

Pros	Job focus	Cons
Example: Getting a job will allow for earning	Focusing on obtaining a job means earning a paycheck immediately	It is possible to get stuck in a job
•	•	•
•	•	•
•	•	•
•	•	•
•	•	•

When it comes to your development as a student with ASD in terms of career goals, opportunities for growth are plentiful in the college context. Taking advantage of resources that are offered to inform you of support and that provide useful information will help you as you make decisions and respond to pitfalls.

Doing the research necessary for graduate school or studying abroad and maintaining positive relationships with faculty and staff at your college who serve as mentors through this process are ways to decrease pitfalls, but pitfalls cannot be avoided entirely. How you define a pitfall or drawback to your progress may change due to your expectations for yourself and the way your life is impacted by unexpected changes and increased demands. How you respond, though, should always be to learn from the pitfall and to try not to repeat it. Learning from experience is the most valuable effort you can put into career exploration as a young adult with ASD, and applying your strengths and skills to the right professional niche can improve your chances of navigating alternate paths in ways that lead to, rather than detract from, your professional success.

BACK TO BASICS

Consider these guiding questions as you prepare to evaluate yourself.

B **Behavior** 1 2 3		Are you considering alternate paths? Have you thought about a graduate degree? Are you exploring career options? Are you monitoring your long- and short-term goals?
A **Academics** 1 2 3		Have you researched graduate programs? Have you thought about studying abroad? Have you explored admission standards to graduate programs you are interested in? Are you applying organizational strategies? Are you engaging in opportunities to help you identify your professional niche?
S **Self-care** 1 2 3		Are you getting enough sleep? Are you eating healthily? Are you planning for your self-care activities? Are you keeping your living space clean? Are you keeping yourself motivated?
I **Interaction** 1 2 3		Are you checking in with your support team? Are you able to communicate your future plans to others? Are you looking for opportunities in your community? Are you talking to those on campus about alternative options?
C **Community** 1 2 3		Do you feel connected? Are you considering others when making your decisions? Are you utilizing your support team to help you get connected? Are you accepting critical feedback? Are you networking in your community?
S **Self-monitoring** 1 2 3		Are you aware of your potential pitfalls? Are you managing your frustration levels? Are you advocating for yourself? Are you realistic about your expectations?

⬇ BACK TO BASICS: RATE YOURSELF

B	**Behavior** 1 2 3	**Comments**
A	**Academics** 1 2 3	**Comments**
S	**Self-care** 1 2 3	**Comments**
I	**Interaction** 1 2 3	**Comments**
C	**Community** 1 2 3	**Comments**
S	**Self-monitoring** 1 2 3	**Comments**

GOALS

Personal:

Academic:

Social:

NEXT STEPS

Preparing for a career takes effort and time. While you are studying in college, your workload can be heavy and the prospect of adding on additional work to prepare for a career can seem impossible, but college is a great place to explore your future goals. As a student with ASD, the structured college setting with its abundant resources can directly help guide you as you identify opportunities for professional growth. Learning about who you are and what your strengths, talents, and skills are is an integral part of the career-readiness process. Many of the academic, social, and independence skills you have learned during your time in college can transfer to the workplace.

Your effort and time preparing for a career can ensure that you end up working toward a desirable long-term career goal, rather than taking the first job you are offered. Considering some of the barriers that individuals with ASD face in the workplace, your next step is to work on utilizing professional tools to navigate these difficult aspects of entering into a career field. Now that you have worked through developing independence, put forth solid effort as a student, and practiced the career preparation methods in this text, your effort should now shift to managing common barriers in the workplace.

BACK TO BASICS CHART STUDENT EXAMPLE

B	**Behavior** 1 2 **3**	**Comments** I have been very engaged in looking for my internship for next semester. I have sent several emails and followed up as well.
A	**Academics** 1 **2** 3	**Comments** I have been struggling in my Calculus II class but have started to use the tutoring center.
S	**Self-care** **1** 2 3	**Comments** I am getting enough sleep and taking care of my living space, but I should work harder on making sure my clothes are always clean.
I	**Interaction** **1** 2 3	**Comments** I spent a lot of time emailing community members about possible job shadowing, but I have not returned any of the phone calls.
C	**Community** 1 **2** 3	**Comments** I attended a career fair for my major and learned a lot about the student organization.
S	**Self-monitoring** 1 **2** 3	**Comments** Even if I am not comfortable talking on the phone, I realize now that I won't be able to set any job shadowing up without returning calls.

GUIDED DISCUSSION

In this appendix, discussion points and guiding questions are offered for each chapter, by lesson. This information is intended to be a starting point for conversation, and should be built on based on the needs of the group, class, or individual. The suggestions are proposed to provoke thought about the material, and we hope that each user will build on these suggestions.

CHAPTER 1: COMPARING INTEREST, TALENTS, AND SKILLS

LESSON 1: INTERESTS VS. SKILLS

DISCUSSION POINTS

Individuals with ASD tend to have very specific and often consuming interests that can both comfort them and make them happy. These interests are topics that they can study and practice tirelessly for hours on end. All too often, however, these individuals are persuaded to stop focusing on these interests and to focus their attention elsewhere. As individuals with ASD begin to start their career search, it may be more valuable to define how those special interests can contribute to their motivation to work through a major and to start a career. When these interests are combined with a well-developed skill set, a person with ASD will have more opportunities to develop a good professional niche.

GUIDING QUESTIONS

- What are some of your interest areas?

- How do your interests motivate you?

- How have your interests changed since becoming a college student?

- In what ways does your special interest contribute to your professional niche?

- How do others perceive you when you are talking about your special interest?

LESSON 2: TALENTS VS. SKILLS

DISCUSSION POINTS

Everybody has specific talents that they are born with. While these talents are innate and often don't require much effort, they can be better developed with practice and commitment. Talents can be viewed through an artistic, athletic, academic, or interpersonal lens, and do not follow a scripted path. Individuals can have talents in just one area, or be equally represented in all four, but everyone has talents that should be respected and developed further. Individuals with ASD should consider these talents as they choose a major and a potential career. When these interests are combined with a well-developed skill set, a person with ASD will have more opportunities to develop a good professional niche.

GUIDING QUESTIONS

- What are some of your identified talents?

- How do talents differ from skills and areas of interest?

- How were these talents developed?

- In what ways have your talents been valuable in your success as a college student?

- What do others say about your talents?

- What category identified in this chapter do your talents fit best in?

LESSON 3: UNDERSTANDING SKILL SETS

DISCUSSION POINTS

Individuals with ASD tend to have very well-developed skill sets that are much narrower than those possessed by their neurotypical peers. These skill sets are most often the skills that are highly desirable in the workforce. For example, people with ASD tend to be very observant of the fine details, and can spend hours focused on tasks. Conversely, the skill set termed "soft skills" can interfere with the ability of people with ASD to be successful in the workforce. The difference between interests, talents, and skills is the amount of work needed to develop skills further. Although "soft skills" may not be strengths, they can be further developed with some commitment. By combining interests, talents, and skills, a person with ASD can find "goodness of fit" within their chosen career, and will have the opportunity to develop a good professional niche.

GUIDING QUESTIONS

- What do you identify as some of your individualized skills?

- How can you see these skills leading to your success?

- What do you see as the major difference between soft skills and career skills?

- What can you commit to in order to develop these skills during the upcoming year?

- Who can you identify as your support team as you work diligently to develop your interests, talents, and skills?

LESSON 4: CREATING BALANCE

DISCUSSION POINTS

By developing a well-balanced approach to infusing interests, talents, and skills to build a professional niche, individuals with ASD can find a career that allows them to achieve both personal and professional satisfaction. The key to establishing this fit is to find a balance between all three prongs. An individual cannot spend too much time focusing on their special interest area and not develop their skill set and expect to have professional success. Conversely, a person cannot spend too much time developing his or her skill set and expect to have personal satisfaction. By identifying strengths in all three areas, an individual can create a career path that is appropriate and has a good potential for success. In addition, being able to discuss this balance fluently will make a person with ASD more marketable to potential employers.

GUIDING QUESTIONS

- What is important about creating a balance between your interests, talents, and skills?

- How can you communicate your interests, talents and skills in a way that others will see as positive contributions?

- How do you plan to continue to develop professionally?

- How do these contribute to your professional development?

- In what ways do you plan to give attention to all three areas?

CHAPTER 2: IDENTIFYING YOUR INDIVIDUAL SKILL SET

LESSON 1: ASSESSING YOUR SKILLS

DISCUSSION POINTS

Companies throughout the country are beginning to purposely seek candidates with ASD because they tend to possess a certain skill set that is viewed as highly sought-after for specific fields. The skills required for efficiency and success can be divided into four distinct skill sets that all have value and can be developed fully. The first step to development, however, is to know where one's baseline is. Self-assessment of skills can give an individual with ASD a starting point to understanding his or her current set of strengths.

GUIDING QUESTIONS

- What skills do you have that would make you a desirable employee?
- How might a better understanding of your skill set help you find more opportunities to grow?
- In what ways have you grown since starting college?
- In what ways do you hope to continue to grow?
- In what way can you commit to strengthening your skill set?
- What did you learn about yourself (from this assessment)?

LESSON 2: DEFINING YOUR SKILL SET

DISCUSSION POINTS

Professional skills can be divided into four distinct sets, all of which are important, and all of which can be developed more fully. A person can have any combination of these skills, but understanding where their skills lie can help develop an understanding of a potential professional niche. These four skill set areas can be defined as analytical, executive function, interpersonal, and leadership skills. Occupations often seek out people with a specific set of skills. This lesson includes an introduction to representative occupations to give people with ASD an indication of potential career choices.

GUIDING QUESTIONS

- What things do you agree with from the results of the assessment?
- What are the results you disagree with?
- Where or in what way might you experience some difficulties?
- How might this contribute to career success?
- Look back to the end of Lesson 2—how do you define your baseline?

LESSON 3: THE CONTINUUM

DISCUSSION POINTS

The four skill sets represented share value and importance within the professional realm, but all too often individuals with ASD have specific skill sets that are remarkable, but have other skill sets that are underdeveloped. This has historically caused difficulties within the workforce for these individuals. Social learning theory has suggested that as people progress through life, experiences may cause these skill sets to shift, but regardless of where strengths lie, they carry tremendous value.

GUIDING QUESTIONS

- Explain how your skill set could transcend across other areas.

- After completing the Skill Set Continuum, what are some things you learned about yourself?

- In what areas did you score the highest? What areas did you score the lowest?

- Did you notice any patterns that emerged while graphing your results? What were they?

- What are some things you can do to fully develop some of your skills?

LESSON 4: CHALLENGE YOUR SKILL DEVELOPMENT

DISCUSSION POINTS

As with any skill, professional skills need to be practiced and constantly developed. With the proper time and commitment to this development, all skill sets can be advanced more thoroughly. Many strategies can be established as a starting point for maturing each skill set, and can range from honing analytical skills through data analysis to furthering executive function skills through defining one's organizational system. As noted previously, all skills, whether a strength or area of development, should be practiced consistently to allow a person with ASD to develop into the most well-rounded professional possible.

GUIDING QUESTIONS

- How do you plan to continue to practice your skill set?

- List some examples of analytical skills you have.

- What do you see as the benefits in building your analytical skills?

- How do you see executive functioning skills contributing to your long-term goals?

- In what ways can you develop your executive functioning skills?

- Why are collaborative skills important in a career, and how can you practice these as a college student?

- How can leadership skills help you in your career?

- How can the act of developing leadership skills help build your confidence?

CHAPTER 3: IDENTIFYING YOUR SKILL SET QUADRANT

LESSON 1: EXPLORING YOUR QUADRANT DIRECTION

DISCUSSION POINTS

Once an individual with ASD has identified his or her specific skill set strengths, analysis can take place to work out how these skills can be used in the work setting. Whether the individual is in a work team or is participating in a group project in school or the community, an understanding about how he or she prefers to use these skills in the group is necessary. The initial preference for many people with ASD is focused on working individually; however, it is necessary to be capable of working as part of a group. Many companies seek potential employees who can work well in collaborative groups, so understanding one's strengths and preferences can allow those with ASD to be successful in this realm while being a strong self-advocate for their preferences. The specific preferences can be separated into two distinct pairs: plan vs. do, and lead vs. connect. Both perspectives within each pair are vital to the success of a group, but an individual's own understanding of his or her preference will allow greater potential for personal and professional success.

GUIDING QUESTIONS

- What role have you taken in a group project?

- How do you see/explain the difference between a "planner" and a "doer"?

- How do you see/explain the difference between "lead" and "connect"?

- How might a team with multiple leaders be impacted when given a task?

- How might an unbalanced team impact success?

LESSON 2: IDENTIFYING YOUR COMPLEMENTARY QUADRANT DIRECTION

DISCUSSION POINTS

To be able to fully experience success in a group setting, individuals with ASD must first recognize that each member of the group has value and brings something to contribute. While individuals with ASD have capabilities and strengths that are very specific, it is vital to also recognize the complementary roles of other potential team members. People in complementary roles possess the capabilities and strengths that are opposite, so these roles, while difficult to manage, produce the best support and can harmonize the team. The roles within any team can be defined as activator, thinker, navigator, and collaborator. Understanding the primary preference and harmonizing role within a team can increase the potential for both individual and team success.

GUIDING QUESTIONS

- How can you value others members of your team?

- What could be challenging about your role within the team?

- How might an activator and navigator pair within a team?

- How might a collaborator and thinker pair within a team?

- Discuss the role of your primary preference.

- What role does your harmonizing ability play when considering teamwork?

LESSON 3: BUILDING YOUR TEAM

DISCUSSION POINTS

For any team to be effective and efficient, it is imperative that all roles, preferences, and skills are equally represented. For instance, if a group has several activators but no navigators represented, the projects would get started quickly, but the group would move aimlessly in several different directions that could result in lack of project completion. Understanding one's own skills, preferences, and roles through this self-evaluation can offer a person with ASD a mechanism to also observe and evaluate the skills, preferences, and roles of other team members. By approaching the analysis of the team members through an analytical research lens, tools can be used to observe, document, and analyze team interaction to best outline these group dynamics.

GUIDING QUESTIONS

- Give an example of a time when you were on a team that did not have a successful outcome.

- What might have been a reason for its successes or failures?

- What are some clues you could utilize to help you see the strengths of others?

- How can you communicate your strengths to others?

- In what way do harmonizing roles create a team balance?

LESSON 4: CAREER EXPLORATION

DISCUSSION POINTS

Young adults with ASD tend to choose potential career paths based on academic success, parental career choices, salary potential, etc., but fail to take into account the motivating factors that make them personally happy. Many factors must be considered when exploring a career, and all should be weighed against each other to evaluate the appropriateness of the chosen field. It is important to consider a field that includes an interest area, but this is not the sole indicator of potential for success. Students must also consider skills, talents, and preferences when considering a potential career. Finally, it is vital for those with ASD to outline the work environment in which they can experience success. For example, if a person prefers to be in a quiet environment due to sensory hypersensitivities, choosing a career in which the final career placement is in a loud workshop would not be considered a good match. All of these considerations can be compared through career exploration brainstorming activities.

GUIDING QUESTIONS

- What careers come to mind while exploring your skill set?

- How can your skill set harmonize with your passion or special interest?

- In what ways can you explore potential career options now that you may have a better understanding of your skill set?

- What specific salary expectations do you have to support your lifestyle choice?

- What environmental indicators are important for you to consider in exploring specific careers?

CHAPTER 4: THE BIG PICTURE OF SUCCESS

LESSON 1: VALUING YOUR JOURNEY

DISCUSSION POINTS

As individuals with ASD progress through the transition from college students to professionals, it is important to understand that the career preparation is a journey that includes several small pieces that combine to form a larger picture. By recognizing that these small pieces are necessary, these individuals can establish consistent techniques to monitor the work needed to progress adequately through this journey. Creating a Skill Development Checkpoint System that is individualized can help keep a person on track towards meeting his or her end goals.

GUIDING QUESTIONS

- What details, if any, did you consider when coming to college?

- What does your big picture plan look like?

- What are some steps you have already taken that contribute to your big picture of success?

- What are some skills you can see as challenging?

- In what ways do you plan to hold yourself accountable?

LESSON 2: CAREER PREPARATION, ONE PIECE AT A TIME

DISCUSSION POINTS

The career preparation process can be viewed in much the same way as a jigsaw puzzle. Each piece has value and fits well with another piece. If one piece is left out, the big picture cannot be complete. While there are 16 common elements in each Career Preparation Puzzle, not every individual will fulfill each piece the same way. Some may choose alternative ways of filling that space, but each space within the larger puzzle will be filled. The elements within the career puzzle can be viewed as not only the pieces of the larger puzzle, but can also be understood as a hands-on resume builder. With the completion of each piece, a portion of the individual's professional resume can be developed as well.

GUIDING QUESTIONS

- What connection can you make with a jigsaw puzzle and your big picture of success?

- Do you have any work-related experience? What did you learn about yourself through that experience?

- What makes you nervous about interviewing for a job or volunteer opportunity?

- Who do you view as a professional mentor?

- What is the value in taking an unpaid internship?

- How can you challenge yourself to focus on the progress rather than the completion of your puzzle?

LESSON 3: MAKING SENSE OF THE PUZZLING DIRECTIONS

DISCUSSION POINTS

Transitions for people with ASD tend to be difficult, which is why it is essential to have a list of resources during this career preparation phase. This process tends to be exploratory by nature, so it can cause some frustration for people if not approached in a methodical way. Preparing for some degree of inevitable ambiguity is recommended during this time. The preparation work that can happen during the preparation phase for not only managing ambiguity but also developing social skills can help people with ASD maintain a professional disposition as they work through the professional decisions they will be required to make.

GUIDING QUESTIONS

- How did your self-exploration help prepare you for your upcoming transition?

- What have you learned about yourself, and how does that play a role in your big picture of successes?

- How can your environment and the influential people in your life contribute to your journey towards success?

- What resources are available to you to help you get clarification through this time in your college career?

LESSON 4: LINKING ACTION AND OPPORTUNITY

DISCUSSION POINTS

As an individual with ASD begins to work through his or her career puzzle, it is vital to keep the big picture in mind. Although the details are essential to work through, the big picture of the career goal is what can be the driving factor to working through the other necessary steps. By examining a personal Career Preparation Puzzle, a person with ASD can identify the pieces that are still missing. These pieces can serve as goals to work through the rest of this journey. The big picture goal should be established first, and then the goals with deadlines for each subsequent piece can be established. From these goals, individuals can establish a prioritized list of action steps to help them navigate through the rest of their career preparation journey.

GUIDING QUESTIONS

- What about this upcoming transition seems overwhelming to you? What do you need in order to feel supported?

- What detailed steps seem the most challenging for you?

- What can you plan to do to help you overcome those challenges?

- How are you prioritizing your action plan?

- What are some realistic deadlines you can set for yourself?

- By taking some of these proactive steps, how could this impact your future career?

CHAPTER 5: REALISTIC CAREER PREPARATION

LESSON 1: EXPLORING THE COLLEGE-TO-CAREER TRANSITION

DISCUSSION POINTS

The transition from college to a career can be closely compared to the transition from high school to college. Just as a person with ASD had to manage the complex process of applying to college, filling out forms, writing essays, and planning for financial aid to enter college, students must take into account many of the same types of tasks in planning a transition into a career. As a college student with ASD, it can be overwhelming to simply manage all the tasks that must be managed to be successful in college. The idea of adding more things to an already vast to-do list may feel unmanageable, but if people with ASD look at the reality of their future through a professional lens, they will notice that it is not entirely different from their existing list. As they restructure their to-do lists to more accurately reflect that of a professional work day, they should take into account optimum work times, potential barriers, preparation times, and options for flexi-time scheduling. By reframing their view of their current to-do lists to reflect that of a professional list, they may notice that the transition will not be all that different from recent transitions they have managed successfully.

GUIDING QUESTIONS

- What steps did you take while transitioning from high school to college?

- How do you expect your responsibilities to change from college to a career?

- What could be some similarities between transitioning into college and transitioning into your career?

- What are some things about your current schedule that might change?

- What are some ways you schedule your academic course load? Will you be able to use the same system?

LESSON 2: NETWORKING POTENTIAL

DISCUSSION POINTS

Although the idea of professional networking can appear daunting to an individual with ASD, with the proper coaching and by developing skills to manage the social nuances, the benefits of networking can be tremendous. College students are situated in a unique environment in which any person with whom they are in contact can eventually become part of their professional network. This plethora of opportunities can serve an individual well if managed appropriately. A very beneficial person to identify to help with the act of networking is a mentor in a student's academic field. This can be a faculty member in the individual's major department who can help them consider the many possibilities in the field. Although the art of networking can be challenging for people with ASD, keep in mind that everyday interactions can lead to potential networking possibilities.

GUIDING QUESTIONS

- What does the phrase "It's not about what you know but who you know" mean to you?

- What might be some of the benefits of reaching out to people you already know?

- How successful have you been at networking as a student?

- Who can you identify as someone you can depend on for guidance?

- What are some personal interactions in the past that have led to opportunities?

LESSON 3: RESUME DEVELOPMENT

DISCUSSION POINTS

As people begin to apply for internship placements or other work possibilities, one of the most essential pieces an applicant can present is a solid resume. This is a very structured document that outlines all relevant information about applicants. There is no universally designed resume template, but most require the same basic sets of information. For the purpose of this lesson, students should gather that information from the Career Preparation Puzzle developed in Chapter 4 to fill in the main three sections of a resume: personal contact information, education history, and work history, taking note of any of the "pieces" that are still blank. These blank pieces can serve as direction for further professional development.

GUIDING QUESTIONS

- How does the lesson on networking relate to this lesson, resume development?

- What might be some advantages to having your resume on hand ready to distribute?

- What are some things about your resume you might want to change when applying for a specific position after college?

- Do you have enough experience to fill one page? If not, what are some steps you could be taking now to fill some of the empty spaces?

- How can you ensure your resume makes you a marketable candidate for a position?

- How do your past experiences relate to your future goals?

LESSON 4: INCREASING YOUR CHANCES

DISCUSSION POINTS

To best increase the opportunities for future career development, the area that individuals with ASD will need to address immediately is the need to be flexible and to develop potential for a professional niche in several arenas. Planning for career preparation is essential, but so is knowing that the plans could go awry, and that they could have to be restructured at any given time. At this point, preparation work for entering a career must be balanced with current academic work. It is important to maintain a good academic standing, as this is a major focus for the initial resume as a person graduates college. In addition, it is important to highlight the specific skills individuals with ASD may already possess, but keep in mind that it is also important to learn new skills that can apply widely to many potential careers. There are many steps to manage, and those with ASD can intentionally take action in preparation for their career that can become overwhelming, but if they develop a visual representation of these tasks, they can manage the process with more ease.

GUIDING QUESTIONS

- What are some sustainable and realistic goals you have identified for yourself?

- What goals are you committed to throughout this coming transition?

- Name some work-related skills you already have.

- What are some ways you could build on those skills to develop additional skills?

- How can you practice the skills you already have?

- What are some potential barriers you might encounter while seeking direction and considering your next steps?

CHAPTER 6: THE INTERVIEW

LESSON 1: SKILL SET AND PREP WORK

DISCUSSION POINTS

As with any undertaking, the job search process takes a lot of planning and sustained effort. There are several steps that must be in place, there are many deadlines that must be met, and the level of time an individual with ASD commits to this process will have a corresponding impact on the outcome of the job search process. It is no longer the case that a job seeker with a degree is first in line for a job. There are now more graduates and qualified applicants for each job available, so the preparation work required for an individual with ASD to rise to the top as the best candidate is growing each year. The best thing to do to prepare for an interview is to research the company and practice interview questions and responses often.

GUIDING QUESTIONS

- What are some ways you practice responding to interview questions?

- What are some things about the interview process that make you uneasy?

- How might the effort you invest in interview preparation reflect on what you get out of the interview experience?

- What are some resources you can identify that will help you find job openings?

- Why is it important to do your research on a company?

- What is the difference between not telling the truth and "marketing" yourself?

LESSON 2: VERBAL AND NONVERBAL BEHAVIOR

DISCUSSION POINTS

During the interview process, it is imperative to present oneself as prepared and professional in both verbal and nonverbal messages with the interviewer. Nonverbal interactions, whether it is the way a person dresses, tone of voice, or eye contact, could potentially have a significant impact on the interview experience. Although the accurate presentation and interpretation of nonverbal behavior is a shared difficulty amongst individuals with ASD, this potential barrier can be overcome with planning and preparation.

GUIDING QUESTIONS

- What are some guidelines to making sure conversation is reciprocal?

- What is a good method for ensuring that you are dressed appropriately for the interview?

- What are some topics you need to be cautious about, including in your responses to questions asked in the interview or the workplace in general?

- Why might it be important to plan ahead when scheduling for an interview?

LESSON 3: TO DISCLOSE OR NOT TO DISCLOSE

DISCUSSION POINTS

The process of making the decision regarding the disclosure of ASD is an art that can only be managed by the individual impacted. This decision does not have a scripted method for determining the best approach, but exists within a grey area. There is no right or wrong method, no right or wrong time for disclosure; it is guided by the interactions and intentions of the individual. There are some strategies available to make the appropriate determination for Why, When, and How to disclose.

GUIDING QUESTIONS

- What might you consider a reasonable accommodation?

- What are the benefits to scripting your own disclosure statement?

- How do you identify proper timing when choosing whether or not to disclose your disability to employers?

- What is a reasonable request to ask of an employer?

- What are some things to avoid when disclosing to your potential employer?

CHAPTER 7: WORK EXPOSURE

LESSON 1: JOB SHADOWING

DISCUSSION POINTS

College students with ASD have many opportunities ahead of them, but just as one would not buy clothing before "trying it on," neither should one enter a career without also "trying it on." Students should identify locations and professionals in their community who are in the career in which they have some interest, leading to a pool of potential people to shadow. To make the most of a job shadowing experience, it is very important to prepare ahead of time. Students should research the company and job to be observed, be prepared to observe and take detailed notes about how the professional interacts with others and conducts daily business, and have a set of questions to ask at the end of the experience. They should be mindful of the time the professional is dedicating to them, and thank them for allowing them to be part of their professional life for the time they were there. As a follow-up, sending a thank you email could leave a lasting impression, and this professional could easily become part of the student's professional network.

GUIDING QUESTIONS

- What are some jobs you would want to "try out"?

- What might be some advantages to job shadowing?

- What are some expectations you have of your future career?

- What would be on your list of things you hope to discover during job shadowing?

- What information can you gain through a company's website?

- What are some topics to avoid when asking questions to professionals already in your field of interest?

LESSON 2: INFORMATIONAL INTERVIEWS

DISCUSSION POINTS

Informational interviews are used to not only gather information about potential careers, but also to make connections within the professional world. These interviews are led by career seekers for the purpose of gathering data about a potential career path, but they can also be used to lend insight into highly sought-after skills and qualifications within the particular company. As a job seeker who is beginning the process of career exploration, it will be helpful to gather information not only about the potential career trajectory, but also information specific to the impact of ASD. Just as with any other interaction with a professional in the community, it is important to carry oneself professionally to leave a lasting impression on this potential networking partner.

GUIDING QUESTIONS

- What might be some benefits to an informational interview?

- What data could be gathered during an informational interview?

- What are some things you need to explore about your ideal work environment?

- How might your professional network benefit you?

- How could you practice your professionalism?

LESSON 3: CAREER FAIRS

DISCUSSION POINTS

Career fairs are events hosted by many colleges to provide an avenue for companies to meet future graduates. These events can be overwhelming for individuals with ASD, but with some strategy, they can also be beneficial. The most overwhelming thing about career fairs is the potential for sensory overload. These events typically take place in a large room, with many tables set up, with representatives from companies having conversations with hundreds of students at a time. By developing a set of guidelines to manage the career fair experience as well as developing a personal sales pitch, a person with ASD can gain the most from the career fair experience.

GUIDING QUESTIONS

- What are some key points to include while introducing yourself at a career fair?

- What are some ways you can prepare for the career fair on your campus?

- What are some appropriate questions to ask during a career fair?

- What types of pre-planning can you do to prepare for a career fair?

- How should you dress at a career fair?

- What might present as a challenge for you at a career fair?

LESSON 4: NETWORKING WITH PROFESSIONALS

DISCUSSION POINTS

Professional networking is a method to expand a sphere of contacts beyond personal daily contacts. The more people that know a person and know of his or her strengths and skills, the greater opportunity he or she will have for getting an interview for a job. Many companies use networking as a method of recruiting potential employees instead of the traditional recruitment strategies. This experience has typically been looked down on by individuals with ASD, because networking tends to be very social in nature; however, new social media sites have been developed just for networking. Developing a professional profile on these social media sites can allow a person with ASD to engage in networking without the need to take part in more social aspects of networking.

GUIDING QUESTIONS

- Who do you have already in your network of professionals?

- What can you identify as ways in which you can network?

- How can you market your skills and interests?

- What can you do to build your profile?

- What types of professionals do you need to be connecting with?

CHAPTER 8: INTERNSHIPS AND STRATEGICALLY PLANNING FOR THE FUTURE

LESSON 1: PROCESS AWARENESS

DISCUSSION POINTS

The process of obtaining and maintaining an internship is similar to the process that is necessary for employment. As such, there are many factors that students with ASD will need to consider about the internship progression in order to determine what the best fit is for both the intern and the company. There are seven steps to the internship progression in this chapter: research, prepare, apply, interview, follow up, commit, and evaluate. Along these seven general steps, students with ASD can design the individual actions steps necessary to move forward along the progression to success at the internship. As students with ASD understand the process, they can focus their attention on preparing for each step.

GUIDING QUESTIONS

- What might you consider when preparing for an internship?

- How might this benefit you?

- What are things to consider when determining "goodness of fit" for an internship?

- What resources are available to you on your campus or within your community to assist you in researching internships?

- Relating to the seven-step progression, how can you plan to prepare?

- What are some internships you might consider applying for?

- How does the information regarding the interview process relate to information in the seven-step progression?

- How can you plan to commit to progress?

- In what ways will you evaluate your success?

LESSON 2: SETTING UP SUPPORT

DISCUSSION POINTS

Internships for college students and young adults are unique because they allow for access to resources available on campus. Setting up support is not only a good idea for young adults with ASD as they enter the internship process, but it is also important to set up support for the internship itself. Having access to campus resources can make this easier, as students can begin with resources like the career center and counseling center to identify potential internship placements that fit their needs and interests, and also to explore how they can be supported during the internship. Students should know how to advocate for themselves, and communicate their needs as they work to gain support. Using a plan to manage internship expectations and reflections, students can work with their supervisor to establish regular practices that support both the student and the internship site.

GUIDING QUESTIONS

- What types of support will you need throughout the internship process?

- Who can you reach out to in order to receive support through this process?

- What connections can you establish that will help you get an internship?

- In what ways are you already advocating for yourself?

- How well do you receive feedback?

- What types of social interactions can you expect to have during your internship?

- In what ways can you effectively communicate with professionals at your internship site?

- How can this lesson actively be used as a guide when communicating your needs to a future internship site or employer?

LESSON 3: RECEIVING FEEDBACK

DISCUSSION POINTS

Students with ASD can utilize feedback about their performance, appearance, and behavior to improve their internship experience. Feedback can be obtained from observing how others react to the student's behavior, or it can be sought after directly. Day-to-day interactions can offer feedback to students with ASD without necessarily labeling it as such, and through formal conversation. Additionally, young adults with ASD may specifically seek feedback about their progress at certain points, gaining situational knowledge, and allowing them to adjust their behavior if necessary. Other feedback comes from the regular, structured, and honest evaluations of supervisors. Compiling feedback and using it to adjust performance and behavior in the internship is an effective way for individuals with ASD to understand their role in the internship company, and how they can better demonstrate their strengths and learn from their mistakes.

GUIDING QUESTIONS

- How can you gain awareness through feedback?

- What social cues are important to remember when receiving feedback?

- Who can you rely on to give you honest and accurate feedback?

- What are some of your own behaviors that might be challenging for you in the workplace?

- How can you create a support plan prior to the internship?

- Why might it be important for you to do self-reflection assessments during this process?

LESSON 4: THE POSSIBILITIES

DISCUSSION POINTS

When students with ASD complete internships, they will have valuable experience to carry forward as they develop their career goals. The possible outcomes depend largely on the input students put into the internship experience. Potential opportunities that students have access to include full- or part-time employment offered at an internship company, advanced professionalism, an increased professional contact network, or the new knowledge that the internship and type of work are not for them. In each of these cases, students with ASD can reinforce their internship experience from the outcome possibilities. Students who take advantage of opportunities like internships not only learn about the job search process, but they also learn "soft skills" in an appropriate and supportive arena to practice them.

GUIDING QUESTIONS

- What are some potential outcomes for your internship?

- What can you identify as future possibilities?

- If you are not offered a job after your internship, what have you learned through the process?

- How has your professionalism developed as a result of your internship?

- Why is it important to consider the successful growth outcomes of the internship process? Describe some social interactions you had through this process, and how they impacted your professional network.

CHAPTER 9: ALTERNATE PATHS

LESSON 1: GRADUATE SCHOOL

DISCUSSION POINTS

Not every college student graduates and immediately enters the workforce. Graduate school, study abroad, job experiences, and building independent living skills are all appropriate options for post-secondary transition as well. Many career paths require advanced degrees however, so young adults with ASD may be required to attend graduate school to best prepare themselves for their chosen career paths. Prior to choosing a graduate school program, it is a student's responsibility to research the programs, entrance requirements, and support available.

GUIDING QUESTIONS

- Does your field of study require a graduate degree or postgraduate training?

- What might be some advantages in obtaining a Master's degree?

- Who can you reach out to in order to get more information about graduate school?

- What schools have programs that align with your field of study?

- How might you have to change your daily schedule when given the additional responsibilities of graduate school?

LESSON 2: STUDY ABROAD

DISCUSSION POINTS

One opportunity that is unique to college students is the ability to study abroad. Whether choosing to take part in a short, cultural immersion trip, or full semester abroad, college students with ASD are encouraged to view this option as a possibility as well. While in college, there are many resources available to support students as they make these decisions. Again, research prior to making a decision is vital, but whichever choice students may make for study abroad, they should know that this experience could have a significant impact on their view of the world and their view of themselves as independent adults.

GUIDING QUESTIONS

- If you could go anywhere in the world, where would you go, and would this be a place you could study abroad?

- Where would you go on your campus to explore the idea of studying abroad?

- What financial obligations would you have if you chose to study abroad?

- What would be the goal of traveling abroad?

- What challenges might you face studying abroad?

LESSON 3: JOB VS. CAREER

DISCUSSION POINTS

While some individuals with ASD choose to graduate college and immediately enter their career path, others choose to enter a job. The main difference between a job and a career is that a job is often a place of employment to develop work skills and to be able to support oneself independently. A career is more strategic in nature, and often develops over time. A career requires discipline and long-term commitment to have the greatest professional impact. Neither choice can be identified as the correct choice for every person, but individuals with ASD should spend time researching the benefits and planning for the best route.

GUIDING QUESTIONS

- How often do you hear the terms "job" and "career" interchanged?

- What is the value of having different jobs before settling into a career?

- What types of jobs could you have that would lead to your ideal career?

- How might a job not related to your career benefit you?

- What is something you are looking for in a long-term position?

LESSON 4: POTENTIAL PITFALLS

DISCUSSION POINTS

Any plan that is put in place by a person getting ready for a transition in life has the potential for pitfalls. Individuals with ASD must be prepared for these pitfalls as they make these life decisions. Although it is natural to want to avoid any potential pitfalls, they are not always negative. For example, one pitfall of entering graduate school after graduation may mean that it takes longer to finish education, but the positive impact would be that the individual would have an advanced degree, which would open up more professional opportunities. It is imperative to also view these potential pitfalls as opportunities, which could have very positive benefits.

GUIDING QUESTIONS

- What might be some of your potential pitfalls?

- What are some alternative paths that you have had to take in the past?

- What would be some potential advantages to deferring your graduation date?

- What could you learn from the pitfalls/mistakes of others?

- In what ways have you seen yourself grow as you have worked through the BASICS College Curriculum?

REFERENCES

Bissonnette, B. (2012) *The Complete Guide to Getting a Job for People with Asperger's Syndrome: Find the Right Career and Get Hired.* London and Philadelphia, PA: Jessica Kingsley Publishers.

Bissonnette, B. (2013) *Asperger's Syndrome Workplace Survival Guide: A Neurotypical's Secrets for Success.* London and Philadelphia, PA: Jessica Kingsley Publishers.

Gabbott, M. and Hogg, G. (2000) 'An empirical investigation of the impact of non-verbal communication on service evaluation.' *European Journal of Marketing 34,* 3, 384–398.

Geither, E. and Meeks, L. (2014) *Helping Students with Autism Spectrum Disorder Express their Thoughts and Knowledge in Writing: Tips and Exercises for Developing Writing Skills.* London and Philadelphia, PA: Jessica Kingsley Publishers.

Grandin, T. and Duffy, K. (2008) *Developing Talents: Careers for Individuals with Asperger's Syndrome and High-Functioning Autism.* Shewanee, KS: Autism Asperger's Publishing Company.

Green, A. (2013) '10 key job search tips for new graduates.' *US News and World Report.* 6 May. Available at http://money.usnews.com/money/blogs/outside-voices-careers/2013/05/06/10-key-job-search-tips-for-new-graduates.

Meyer, R.N. (2001) *Asperger Syndrome Employment Workbook: An Employment Workbook for Adults with Asperger Syndrome.* London and Philadelphia, PA: Jessica Kingsley Publishers.

Niles, S.G. and Harris-Bowlsbey, J. (2009) *Career Development Interventions in the 21st Century, 3rd edition.* Upper Saddle River, NJ: Pearson.

Rigler, M., Rutherford, A., and Quinn, E. (2015) *Developing Identity, Strengths, and Self-Perception for Young Adults with Autism Spectrum Disorder: The BASICS College Curriculum.* London and Philadelphia, PA: Jessica Kingsley Publishers.

Simone, R. (2010) *Asperger's on the Job: Must Have Advice for People with Aspergers.* Arlington, TX: Future Horizons.

Walsh, L., Lydon, S., and Healy, O. (2014) 'Employment and vocational skills among individuals with Autism Spectrum Disorder: Predictors, impact, and interventions.' *Journal of Autism and Developmental Disorders 1,* 4, 266–275.

INDEX

14 Day Loan

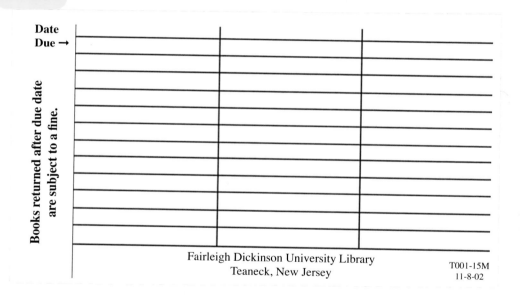

Date Due →

Books returned after due date are subject to a fine.

Fairleigh Dickinson University Library
Teaneck, New Jersey

T001-15M
11-8-02